# SEEDS
# MY FATHER
# PLANTED

*The Garden He Cultivated In Me*

*A Memoir*

## BY GILDA WRAY

WRAY OF LIGHT PUBLISHING

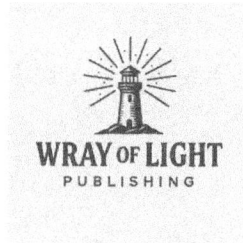

**WRAY OF LIGHT**
PUBLISHING

Published by Wray of Light Publishing
Lacey, WA, USA

Email: gildawray@tuta.com

First Edition

ISBN: 978-1-968631-07-9

Printed in the United States of America

# Dedication

To my father,
D.J.B.,
who planted seeds of love
that bloom eternal

# A Garden Worth Remembering

This is the first Father's Day without my dad.
The first time I can't pick up the phone to hear his voice,
or listen to one of his wildly imaginative stories,
or talk about the books we were reading together—
something we did every day.

I don't recall a day I didn't speak with my father.
He always wanted me to write a book.
This is my promise to him—kept.
He believed words matter
because people matter.
He taught me that what we plant
in one another
can grow long after we're gone.

This book is my offering.
Not a perfect memoir, but a living garden—
a place where the seeds he
planted in me,
through laughter, stories,
guidance, and quiet sorrow,
have taken root.

Some sprouted early.
Some lay dormant for years.
Some are only now blooming—
watered by grief and grace in
equal measure.

These pages hold fragments of the garden
my father cultivated in me and in others—
seeds he sowed quietly across decades
of gentle presence and delight.

He had this uncanny ability
to make whoever he was with
feel like his absolute favorite
person in the world.

To sit with my father—even for a moment—
was to be known, delighted in,
and often gifted a parable
woven seamlessly into casual conversation.

These reflections are my recollections—
told the way I remember them.
And memory, as you know, isn't always perfect.
But it is perfectly ours.

Like a diamond held to the light,
each memory shines differently depending on the angle.
My family—and all who knew
him—
may hold different facets of the same stories.
And all of them are true.
All of them are him.

This book isn't just about my father.
It's about what he cultivated.
It's about love that shows up in early mornings,
in whispered lessons,
in oddly timed jokes,
in quiet sacrifices,
and in the roots we don't realize are there
until we need them to hold us.

If you, too, are walking through the ache
of remembering someone you love,
I pray these pages offer you
shade, and scent, and soil.

Because maybe what we
remember
isn't only what was,
but what's still growing.

May you find the roots that hold you firmly.
And may you be held.
And may you never forget
that your words, like seeds, are
still becoming.

Come walk the garden he planted with me.

# Table of Contents

"What do you see?" he'd ask.
And somehow, I'd always see more.

# WINTER

CHAPTER 1

# When Letters Walk Together

The first seed my father planted grew into my understanding of connection itself. He taught me that letters, like people, are meant to walk together—and in that walking, they create meaning. This is how I learned to read both words and the world.

"Books are doorways. Letters are people. Stories are how we learn to walk together."

I was a shy child.

In crowded rooms, at family gatherings, in unfamiliar countries or cultures, I often sought refuge behind my father's legs, small hands clutching the fabric of his pants as though they were a shield. The world felt too loud, too large, too unknown.

And that's exactly where my father met me—in that shyness. Not to pull me out of it, but to walk me through it.

## The Lesson

He taught me to read when I was just three years old. Not only in English—but also in Italian. But what he really taught me was something much deeper. To him, reading was not a skill—it was an invitation.

He began with vowels.

"Vowels are great friends," he told me. "When they walk alone, they speak their true sound when meeting other letters. But when two vowels walk together, the first vowel is brave and says its name out loud while the second vowel stays quiet because it's shy. The brave one protects the shy one."

He grinned. "Just like when a dog is by himself, he says 'woof'—that's his sound. But when you and the dog are together, you don't just hear his bark—you call his name: 'Here, Buddy!' The sound becomes a name when friends walk together."

And so, letters had both sounds and names. And when they walked together, they didn't just bark—they began to speak.

He explained that when letters walk together—as friends often do—they form words.
When words walk together, they form meaning.
When meanings walk together, they form sentences.
When sentences walk together, they form stories.
And when stories walk together—they create worlds.

Then he looked at me and said, "We are like letters, too. We have names. We make sounds. When we walk together in kindness and attention, we create meaning. We create stories. We create worlds."

He never rushed the lesson. He made it playful and full of awe. He'd introduce letters to me like new friends. "This is A," he'd say. "She's always singing. And this is B—he's a little bouncy." Then he'd show me how they strolled across the page together, hand in hand.

But he didn't stop there.

He bent down to my level, gently moving me from behind his legs, and said, "You don't need to be afraid. People are just like letters, too."

I blinked at him, unsure.

"Every person," he said, "is like a letter walking through the world. We each carry our own sound, our own purpose. And just like letters form words when they come together, people form relationships, ideas, and communities. They form meaning."

He paused, letting that settle.

"If you pay attention to each 'letter,' you'll learn new stories. You'll walk into new worlds. You'll understand that people aren't something to fear… they're something to read. Something to know."

With that, my father gave me a way to belong—even in a room full of strangers.

I didn't know it then, but he taught me that behind every face is a story, and behind every story, a world waiting to be discovered.

He also taught me that words held a quiet power. A sacred responsibility.

"It matters how we use them," he'd say, with a kind of seriousness that made even my young heart still. "Words can build a beautiful world, full of life and love—or they can create a dark one, full of sorrow and pain."

To him, it wasn't just grammar or vocabulary. It was creation. Every person, as an individual "letter," speaks and adds something to the larger story we are all part of. We are not just passing through—we are authoring the world with our presence, our tone, our language, our kindness—or lack of it.

From him, I learned to see the wonder of each person— their importance in their own small sphere, and in the vast tapestry of the larger world. He made it clear: words are not throwaway things.
They are sacred.
They are living.
They are the language of being.

I learned to cherish the preciousness of words, and the sacredness of the language of being.

But he didn't just teach me to see people as letters—he showed me how stories themselves could be discovered in countless ways.

One of the first books we explored together was In A People House by Dr. Seuss.

At three years old, I was mesmerized by the pictures—the strange creatures, the colorful rooms, the parade of items and activities spilling across each page. But before I could even see the cover, he took me on a different kind of journey.

We sat together and turned through the book, page by page, studying the images without reading a single word aloud. He asked me what I saw. What I thought might be happening. What the story could be, just from the pictures alone.

Then, with a quiet smile, he flipped the book upside down and asked, "Now that you've seen all the pictures, what do you think this book is about?"

I don't remember exactly how I answered. But I remember how it felt: like he was letting me discover the story myself. Like my guesses mattered. He offered a few of his own ideas, too—some funny, some wild, all full of curiosity.

Then came the question: "Do you think our ideas are good ones?"

Only after we shared did he finally reveal the cover. We looked at the real title. We compared it to our own. We laughed at how close—or how far—we'd been.

And then he said something I'll never forget:

"The author gave the book a title. But our titles worked too. Because even if we all see the same thing, it can mean something different to each of us—and still be just as right, just as real."

That was the day he began teaching me that people are the same.

"Your mother," he said, "is Mommy to you and your siblings. But to me, she's my wife. To her parents, she's their daughter. To her brothers, she's a sister. All those names are different, but they all describe the same person. All are true."

In this gentle way, he started to help me overcome my fear of new people, new places, new names. He showed me how to see people not as strangers, but as stories—many-layered, familiar, meaningful.

That day, sitting beside him and reading without reading, I learned something much bigger than the story in the book.

I learned how to see.

## *The Understanding*

And I learned something else too—something that would echo in my life again and again:

Words hold power.

This, my father taught me, was a gift that everyone shares. The way we use this incredible power can create a world full of harmony and joy. Or, used carelessly, it can form a world of sorrow and pain.

He taught me to listen carefully—not just with my ears, but with my heart.

The silences between syllables.
The stories behind the voices.
The emotion hidden in the rhythm.

"Every person," he'd say, "is a letter walking through the world. Pay attention to what words they're speaking. What would you call the story they are writing?"

Because only by paying attention could I understand the ways I might enter someone else's story. Not to take over. But to walk beside.

If I saw someone smile, he would gently lean down and ask, "What do their eyes tell you? What do you feel? Do their eyes match what you feel?" He was teaching me to notice subtleties, to hear beyond the spoken word, to recognize the language behind the language.

And in that noticing, something softened in me. What once felt overwhelming—faces, voices, rooms full of unknowns—began to shimmer with curiosity. People felt less like noise and more like beautiful meaning.

I began to see joy instead of strangers.
I began to understand that what looked like anger was often just fear.
Or passion.

Sometimes even love—a love someone didn't know how to show.

He bent down often in those early years, when I would hide behind him, afraid of being seen. But he never told me not to be afraid. He didn't dismiss my fear.

Instead, he would ask, "What are you afraid of?"

And then, quieter still:

"I don't mean what you see. Look inside yourself. What do you feel that makes you afraid?"

Even as a tiny girl, I could begin to understand that what I was most afraid of... was being seen.

To be seen for myself.

And he would look me in the eyes with such calm and say,
"It's good to understand that you are precious.

And sometimes... we need to show others what preciousness sounds like in a story."

Looking back, I can see that it was in that very realization—being seen for myself—that something permanent awakened in me.

Because that... that was what I felt when my father looked at me.

He didn't just see my face. He saw my why.
He saw my heart. He saw my inner landscape. He saw the questions my heart didn't yet know how to ask.

And in the space between us, I saw him too.

When I looked into his eyes, when I watched his face, the way he moved through the world, I saw that he felt as deeply as I did.

But he walked more bravely.

He carried the same weight of feeling—but he carried it like light.

And somehow, he lit the way for me.

He would often ask me what I thought the "letters" are saying—what story they were writing with their words, their eyes, their presence.

And then, he would ask me something even more important:

"Is there anything you would like to say to join their story?"

Or, "What story would you like to write alongside them?"—and "How would you walk with them along their path?"

I didn't know it then, but he was teaching me the sacred art of walking with others—of reading the world not with judgment, but with wonder.

This seed he planted—that people are letters walking together—would grow into every relationship I'd ever form.

And in every word I now write, I'm still walking with him.
He taught me that I wasn't just a reader of life.

I was a participant.
I was a letter, too.

And the way I spoke, the way I moved, the way I loved—
it all mattered.

## *The Inheritance*

*Letters Walk Together Still*

Years later, I would understand the full depth of what he'd given me. In his last years, while he was sick, I reminded him how he taught me to read.

He seemed surprised.

"I told you that about vowels?"

"Yes," I said. "That's how I taught my children. And now, I tell this to my grandchildren."

He made that thoughtful little sound—his thinking sound—and then said, "Well... what do ya know."

I told him he was a paradox to his own lesson. In his story, the brave vowel speaks its name. But he walked through the world bravely and protected the shy one beside him.

And yet—he never said his own name out loud.

He carried his true sound silently, but it was felt.
He carried others' sounds.
He gave space.

He made room.
He was both letters at once—
which doesn't work in phonics or grammar…
but it worked in what he would later call his "elastic dream machine world"—a place where contradictions could coexist beautifully, where impossible things became everyday magic.

A world he was teaching me to inherit, one letter at a time.

# CHAPTER 2

# The Listening Game

The second seed my father planted taught me that stories live everywhere—not just in books, but in the music people choose, the books they keep, the rhythms they move by. He showed me how to listen for the invisible stories that surround us.

My father believed that stories were never confined to books.
They were tucked into record players, behind coffee mugs,
woven into the corners of a bookshelf,
and sometimes,
whispered through the music someone left playing in the other room.

He taught me to listen not just with my ears,
but with curiosity.

When I was small and timid—especially when we had to visit people I didn't know—he would make a game of it.
"Let's see who can find the bookshelves first," he'd say with a wink.
"And the music. That matters, too."

It felt like a secret mission.
While others made small talk or stood awkwardly in doorways,
we quietly scanned the room.
And sure enough—there it would be.

A modest stack of well-loved paperbacks.
A row of biographies.
Maybe a shelf with science, classics or poetry.
Or cookbooks or books on art and architecture.

"There," he'd whisper. "Now we know something about them."
And suddenly, the mystery of the person would begin to unfold.

He never taught me to judge what they read—only to wonder.
"Someone who reads mysteries," he once said,
"might be someone who's still solving a few of their own."
"Someone who loves poetry," he mused another time,
"likely hears music in the world the way we do."

We'd listen for music, too.
Not just what was playing through the speakers,
but the kind that hummed in the way someone spoke,
or the way a room felt when they smiled.
He said every person has their own soundtrack.
"And if you can hear it," he told me, "you'll know how to move with them."

What felt like a simple game was actually changing everything.
I stopped fearing new places.
I started listening—really listening.
To the stories people weren't saying.
To the books they cherished.
To the rhythms they moved by.

And eventually,
I began to feel like I belonged—like I was part of the story, too.
Like I was stepping into a book that was still being written—
and I got to help write it.

I didn't know it then, but my father was giving me
the tools to see the invisible.
To hear the unheard.
To understand people not just by what they say—
but by what they love.

This chapter of my life began as a game.
But it became a way of seeing.
A way of being.

"Bookshelves and background music," he once told me,
"are like footprints people leave behind without realizing it.
Follow them gently, and they'll often lead you straight to someone's
heart."

He also believed music could be a translator.

"If you're ever somewhere you don't know the language," he told me,
"don't panic. Just listen to the music.
How does it make you feel?
What colors do you see in your mind?
That will show you how to move with the people there."

He developed this listening even deeper still. We played a game, just
the two of us.
He would put on music from around the world—
a Celtic reel, a solemn symphony, a lively jazz piece—
and I had to choose how to dress the music.
Not in costume, but in feeling.

"This one sounds like a celebration," he'd say.
"Not funeral clothes!"
Or, "This one's sleepy—no bright colors now."

Sometimes I'd run for scarves and twirl to match the beat.
Other times I moved slowly, almost reverently, letting the notes guide
my body.

And sometimes we played in reverse.
He'd pick an outfit or a mood, and I had to find the music that
matched.

It wasn't about being right.
It was about listening.
And feeling.
And trusting that stories can speak through rhythm,
if you let them.

## *Footprints of Grace*

Looking back, I understand that some lessons are too deep for words.
They live in sound, in movement,
in the way a child picks up a scarf
and somehow knows:
this song needs blue.

Some stories don't begin with language.
They begin with listening—
to drums that feel like home,
to flutes that flutter like questions,
to the hush between two chords
where something holy waits.

Years later, I would fully grasp that my father knew that music carries
meaning when words fail.
That every culture has a heartbeat.

That grief hums low, and joy dances,
and longing sometimes plays itself
as a single violin in an empty room.

He taught me to listen
with my eyes,
with my fingertips,
with my soul.

To follow the trail of tones
like breadcrumbs back to the heart of a stranger.

And to never be afraid
of a language I don't yet understand—
because music, if I listen closely, will always show me how to speak.

This seed he planted—that listening reveals the invisible stories around
us—would grow into my ability to find connection anywhere, with
anyone. All I had to do was listen for their music.

# CHAPTER 3

# Words Create Worlds

In the winter of my understanding, the third seed my father planted would teach me about the sacred power of words themselves. This lesson came not in our living room or through a book, but in the quiet cathedral of my grandmother's woods.

I was probably seven or eight when my father gave me one of the most important lessons of my life. We were walking together in my grandmother's woods—one of my favorite places to explore with him. I don't remember exactly what I'd said or done, but I'm sure I was being feisty or hasty with my words, probably with my siblings. I loved having him to myself on these walks and didn't want to share his attention.

Suddenly, he stopped walking.

It was as if every bird stopped singing. The wind stopped. Everything got very quiet—that kind of profound stillness that makes a child's heart pause.

He looked directly into my eyes with a gravity I'd never seen before.

"Choose your words very carefully," he said. "And mark how you deliver them. Words create worlds. They bring flourishing or destruction. They are one of our greatest powers. And once spoken you cannot simply take them back.

You can apologize, but they are never gone. Sound travels. They continue.

People may not remember what you've said. But they will remember how you have made them feel. And the words—their sound and the weight of them—continue to travel further and further into space.

You have this power to bring love and life and beauty," he said. "Use it wisely and well."

The gravity of his words created a kind of reverent hush in me. I can still see his face, still feel the weight of that moment in those quiet woods. He must have noticed my wide eyes because he quickly added, "I'm not saying this to frighten you, sweetheart. I'm saying it to encourage you.

For with great gifts and great power comes great responsibility. Knowledge helps us to wield these well. That's all."

## Reflection

Years later, I would understand the full weight of what he taught me that day:

Words shape more than sentences.
They shape souls.

We speak, and something moves—within us, and within others.

A word of kindness becomes a shelter.
A harsh phrase, a scar.

But when we speak with love, when we slow down and choose with care, our words can plant gardens.
They can restore what was broken.
They can bear fruit long after we are gone.

Maybe that's why my father's words echo still.
Not because they were loud.
But because they were true.
And he lived them.

I often think of times when someone's words changed me—for better or for worse. And I consider the last words I spoke today. What world did they create? What would it look like to speak as if every word carried eternal weight—not in fear, but in reverence?

Speak love.
Shape life.
The world is listening.

This seed he planted—that words create worlds—would grow into my understanding that every conversation is an act of creation. Every word I speak is a choice to build up or tear down, to plant gardens or scatter stones. In the cathedral of those woods, he taught me that language itself is sacred.

# CHAPTER 4

# The Banana Is Not Me

In the winter of my understanding, the fourth seed my father planted would teach me the difference between having an opinion and being that opinion. This lesson would save me from countless conflicts and help me see that most disagreements aren't really about the thing we're arguing about at all.

## *The Lesson*

The moment my brothers' voices started rising—
"My toy is the coolest!"
"No, mine is better!"—
Dad would appear with that mischievous glint in his eye, like he was about to reveal a magic trick.

"Oh really? When did you become a toy?"

That one sentence deflated the whole thing.
We'd laugh.
He'd help us sort out what we were really saying.
It always sounded sillier when we heard it out loud.

Soon, we started creating fake arguments on purpose—
"My toy is smarter than your toy," "Well, my toy has a license to fly"—
just to hear Dad chime in:
"Oh? And when did you become a pilot?"

It was hilarious.
And brilliant.

I didn't realize until decades later that my father had given us a master key—not just for childhood squabbles, but for every human conflict I'd ever encounter.

## *The Understanding*

What I came to understand was that disagreements aren't always opposites—they're often different faces of the same truth, each person seeing their own angle of something larger than both of them.

To one person, a banana is pure sunshine—sweet, tropical, perfect. To another, it's absolutely revolting—mushy, cloying, wrong in every way. One person feels the smooth skin first. Another notices the fuzzy texture that makes them shudder. One tastes the flavor immediately. Another experiences the texture before anything else.

But it's still a banana.

No one is wrong.
No one is entirely right.
The banana just… is.

And all is well—if we can see that the banana is not me.
That's where things go sideways.

When someone critiques the banana and I mistake it as a critique of me—that's when the problem begins.

We weave the banana into our identity—make it part of our story, our worth, our very sense of self.

And when we do, conflict is not far behind.

My dad understood this instinctively—the way some people understand music or mathematics. He could spot the moment when someone confused the thing with themselves.

## *The Application*

Years later, this lesson would shape how I navigate every disagreement. Now, when I see someone afraid to express their favorite team or viewpoint, I encourage them. When I see others being argumentative about preferences, I gently remind them: these are not identities but expressions of delight. Gifts in the world. Opportunities to learn from one another. To experience joy through another's lens.

A favorite sports team is not a personal declaration against you any more than it is for me.

Just as flowers do not deny the field but brighten it. The field creates a beautiful canvas for the flowers. They are synergistic.

One person enjoys and sees the flowers first.
Another notices the field.
Both are beholding beauty—just different aspects of the same gorgeous landscape.

Most of the time, we're all trying to get to the same place:
To be heard.
To be known.
To be respected.

We just go about it differently.

But if we can pause long enough to remember the banana is not me, and help each other along the way, how much better the journey becomes.

This seed he planted—that we are not our preferences—would grow into my ability to disagree without being disagreeable, to have strong opinions without making them into identity wars. In a world that seems determined to turn every difference into a battle, maybe we all need to remember:

The banana is just a banana.
The flowers are just flowers.
The field is just a field.

We are so much more.

# SPRING

# When Spring Speaks

Spring has always felt like a whisper from Heaven—
soft and surprising, full of reminders that life is still being made
new.

My father loved spring.
He marveled at its colors,
paused to savor its scents,
and found parables tucked into every blooming thing.

This season, my first spring without him beside me,
has spoken louder than I expected.

It has called to me
through yellow weeds,
red blossoms,
hummingbird wings,
and even the absence of a familiar whine.

And in all of it,
I hear him still.
Teaching me.
Laughing with me.
Feeding me.

# CHAPTER 5

# The Birthday Gift

As spring awakened around me, the fifth seed my father planted began to bloom in my understanding. This was a lesson about gratitude—not just feeling it, but actively expressing it in ways that honor the gift of life itself.

My father was always special.

Even as a young boy, he carried a deep sense of gratitude—and he found ways to show it. One year, still just a lad, he began a tradition that would last a lifetime. Instead of expecting a gift on his birthday, he decided he would give one. He wanted to thank his mother for giving him life.

To earn the money, he asked his uncles if he could help out on their dairy farm. It was a bold offer from such a small boy, but he was earnest. Most mornings, well in advance of his birthday, he joined them. Though the work was far beyond his years, they found ways to include him.

He always laughed when he told me the story. "Truth is, I didn't do much of anything," he'd say. "Mostly just rode around in the dairy truck." But then his smile would soften as he remembered the words that stayed with him all his life:

"Boy! I sure am glad you came along to help me today. I would've been talking to myself all day if you hadn't come!"

That encouragement made him feel like he mattered. That he could help. That he belonged.

And he did help. He earned just enough to buy a postcard—a beautiful nature scene he'd picked out with care, knowing how much his mother loved the outdoors. That card, given over a birthday breakfast, began a tradition between mother and son that they would keep for a lifetime.

Each year, they shared a birthday breakfast together. Each year, he honored the one who gave him life with a gift of his own.

I didn't fully grasp then how this story would shape me, but he adored his mother. And I believe it was in these early mornings and quiet gestures that his own gift of gentleness was born. He would spend the rest of his life making people feel seen, included, and quietly celebrated—just like his uncles did for him, and just like he did for her.

## *Reflection*

Looking back, I can see how this tradition revealed something profound about the way my father moved through the world. Some people give because it's expected. Others give because they want to be seen.

But the rarest kind of giving flows from a soul that simply understands the sacredness of love and life.

My father's tradition of giving a birthday gift to his mother wasn't just charming—it was prophetic. It shaped how he moved through the world: seeing others, honoring them, and never letting love go unspoken.

What I came to understand was that he carried this same spirit everywhere he went. In grocery store lines, he'd notice the tired cashier and offer a genuine compliment. With waitresses, he'd remember their names and ask about their families. He planted seeds of worth in strangers, just as his uncles had planted them in him.

This seed he planted—that life itself is a gift worth celebrating by giving back—would grow into my own understanding of gratitude. But more than that, it would help me recognize that this same seed lives dormant in everyone, waiting for the right moment to sprout.

I've never met anyone else who gave birthday gifts to their mother. But I wonder—what seed of gratitude might be stirring in you right now? What life-giver in your world might be waiting for a simple acknowledgment that their love mattered?

The beautiful truth is that my father's seeds weren't just planted in me. They were scattered everywhere he walked, in every person he made feel seen. And now, perhaps, one might be taking root in you.

# CHAPTER 6

# The Cherry Tree and the Skating Pond

As spring continued to unfold, the sixth seed my father planted began to reveal itself—not through a specific lesson, but through the way he carried joy. This was a lesson about remembering: that the goodness we've known can become a lens for seeing goodness still possible.

My father loved his childhood.

He spoke of it often—not as a list of memories, but as a living world he could still enter. A world of muddy boots and laughter. Of street corners where every neighbor knew your name. Of summer evenings spent chasing fireflies and winter nights skating by torchlight.

He grew up surrounded by family—real family and the kind you make when neighbors become kin. His uncles ran dairy farms, and he was happiest tagging along, bouncing in their trucks and feeling important just to be included. He also spent time helping his grandparents on their gardening farm—planting flowers, watering rows, and learning the quiet rhythms of growth.

But one memory always stood out.

His favorite person of all was his grandmother on his mother's side. She was feisty and wore pants when it wasn't considered proper. A rebel in the best kind of way.

He would watch, mesmerized, as she sat each evening and unbraided her long white hair, then re-braided it for bed. There was something sacred in the rhythm of it. Something wild and free, and yet entirely composed.

Each afternoon, she would take him upstairs to her room, where their secret awaited. Quietly, they'd open the window, slip through like adventurers, and leap hand-in-hand off the roof—straight into the arms of their favorite cherry tree. Just the two of them, perched among branches heavy with fruit, eating cherries and telling stories.

It was magic.
And he never outgrew it.
Family was everything to him.
So were neighbors. So was beauty.

In the wintertime, when the pond in their backyard froze over, the entire town would gather. Families placed benches and food stands around the edge, and children would skate while their parents laughed and sipped warm drinks together. It was simple. Ordinary. Holy.

Whenever he spoke of it, there was a look in his eyes—wistful, far-off, and full of joy. The kind of joy you can't fabricate. The kind of joy that lives deep inside a person and becomes the lens through which they see the world.

Sometimes I would ask him, "Could it really have been like that? Just a few decades ago?"

He would smile—but never answer.
Because maybe he didn't have to.
Maybe he just wanted me to picture it. To feel it.
To believe that such goodness was possible.

I didn't realize then that he wasn't just sharing memories—he was teaching me to see the world through the eyes of wonder, to believe that beauty and community and simple joy weren't just relics of the past, but possibilities for the present.

## *Reflection*

Looking back, I can see how it's easy to forget that goodness once filled the cracks of everyday life. But when someone tells a story with reverence, it can do more than just preserve the past—it can awaken something inside us.

My father didn't just remember his childhood.

He re-membered it—stitched it back together through story and delight, inviting us to step into it with him.

What he was really teaching me was that when we remember with reverence, we don't just preserve the past—we plant hope for the future. We create a vision of what's possible when people choose connection over isolation, wonder over cynicism, joy over resignation.

This seed he planted—that joy is a choice and wonder is a way of seeing—would grow into my own ability to find magic in ordinary moments. He showed me that we can be the ones who re-member what mattered, who carry it forward not as nostalgia, but as hope.

Maybe that's the invitation for all of us now. Not to replicate the past—but to recover what it gave: a sense of belonging, of beauty in simplicity, of wonder that finds its way into cherry trees and frozen ponds.

And perhaps, in the re-membering, we discover that such goodness isn't just possible—it's still being written, one story at a time.

# CHAPTER 7

# The Lesson of the Weeds

As spring painted the roadsides with brilliant yellow, the seventh seed my father planted came rushing back to me. This was a lesson about attention—about the difference between what grows wild and what we choose to cultivate.

Every spring of my childhood, as we drove past those splashes of brightest yellow running alongside the road—like cheering friends, calling out greetings along the way—I would smile and ask my father what they were called.

And each time, with a little chuckle, he would remind me: "They're not actually flowers, you know. They're weeds."

Was it broom bush?
I think that was the name.

Still, I called them beautiful.
And each year, he reminded me to remember their lesson.

"Weeds," he said, "grow fast.
They don't need a gardener to plant them,
or water them, or care for them.

They only need a lazy gardener—
one who either isn't paying attention
or doesn't really care about the fruit they meant to grow."

He never said it unkindly.
He said it as one who had spent time in gardens—
and in life.

"Good gardeners," he told me,
"expect weeds.
They're not surprised by them.
They don't shame themselves when they appear.
They just tend their gardens."

"They look for them each day,
before the roots dig in too deep.
Not to obsess—
but to protect what they intentionally planted.
Because fruit takes time.
It takes tending.
It grows slower, but it feeds and strengthens.

"Weeds grow fast.
They may look lovely,
but they don't nourish.
They crowd.
They steal.
But that also makes them easy to spot."

And then he'd say something like this—
"Don't be discouraged by the weeding.
It's the weeding—not just the planting—
that makes a fruitful garden grow.

Pay attention,
and your garden will bear good fruit."

As a child, I would often sigh and protest,
"I just wanted to know its name!"

But what I came to realize was that he heard more than my question.
He heard the seed of wonder beneath it.
And he answered not only with a name,
but with a story that would one day feed me again.

I didn't understand then that this lesson would become one of the most practical gifts he ever gave me. Years later, this wisdom would help me recognize the difference between what deserves my attention and what simply demands it—between the relationships worth tending and the distractions that crowd them out.

This seed he planted—that life requires intentional tending—would grow into my understanding that we must choose daily what we want to cultivate. In relationships, in habits, in the thoughts we allow to take root, the principle remains the same: good fruit requires good gardening.

**P.S.**

While writing this chapter,
I finally realized it wasn't "broom brush" at all—
it was "scotch broom."
After decades of mishearing him!

Just days earlier, I'd wondered about an old email
where he mentioned someone with a "scotoma"—
a blind spot.

Turns out, I was the character all along.

Even in memory, Dad's still teaching me to pay attention.

Some lessons take a lifetime to fully hear.

# CHAPTER 8

# The Whine of Spring

In my first spring without him,
the eighth seed my father planted
revealed itself not through his presence,
but through his absence.

This was a lesson about different ways of blooming—
and how love continues to teach us
even when the teacher is gone.

This spring, as I walked the paths we used to share,
I found myself remembering
how my father used to love to meander around
and marvel at all the colors and smells.

Often, we would each take a book with us
and find a place to sit—
usually wherever the scent was so delicious
it called us to pause.

Reading like that never worked well.
We constantly interrupted each other.
"Ohhh, listen to this!" he'd say.

Or, more often from me,
"Hey—what do you think this means?"
I used to think we should just bring one book to share.

But I was never patient enough to sit and wait
while he read
and I sat empty-handed.

So, here I am.
My first spring without my father by my side.

I came around a bend and there,
within a sea of green,
was the most magnificent splash of red—
gigantic blossoms reaching high into the sky.

A rhododendron in full glory.
I stopped in my tracks,
marveling aloud…
And then I realized how silly I must have looked
to anyone watching.

Because I was talking—
to no one.
Or rather,
I was talking to him.

How I miss having him there
to wonder with me.
To delight in the simplest things.

As I stood there talking to the air,
I found myself listening for something else I'd grown to love—
the familiar whine of his electric scooter.

It whined.

And the faster he went,
the louder it got.

He would forget that my legs weren't very long
and couldn't keep up
with his high-speed cruising.

What I wouldn't give
to hear that whine beside me again.

As I stood before the towering red blossoms,
exclaiming aloud to no one in particular,
I paused and asked myself—
What would he say in return?

I could hear him,
clear as spring air:

"What a beauty!

Just remember, though—
the ones that show off their beauty
often fade the fastest.

They blossom big and bright…
but before you know it,
they're just green again like the rest."

And we would laugh.

I'd say,
"When have I ever been a show-off?"

And he'd grin,
"Well… it's nice to see once in a while."

Then he'd add—
"The key is remembering we all bloom.

We bloom at different times
and in different ways.

Sometimes in a riot of color.

And sometimes
in just remaining still…
and being."


## *Reflection*

Standing there,
hearing his voice so clearly in my memory,
I realized this seed he planted—
that we all bloom in different ways and seasons—
had taken root deeper than I knew.

Some people bloom in riots of color,
demanding attention.

Others bloom quietly,
in the simple act of remaining present,
of being.

And some,
like my father,
continue blooming even after they're gone,

their wisdom flowering
in the hearts of those they loved.

What I came to understand
was that his lessons weren't confined to the years we shared.

They live on
in every spring walk,
every moment of wonder,
every conversation I have
with the world around me.

The whine of his scooter may be silent now,
but his voice—
gentle, wise, delighting in beauty—
continues to bloom
in every spring conversation
I have with the world around me.

This seed he planted
would grow into my understanding
that love doesn't end with absence—
it transforms.

It becomes the voice we hear in memory,
the wisdom that guides us forward,
the way we continue to bloom
even when we think we're walking alone.

# CHAPTER 9

# He Taught Me to See

As spring deepened around me, the ninth seed my father planted began to bloom in my understanding. This was a lesson about seeing—not just looking, but truly beholding the world as sacred text, written by the Author of all things.

## *The Seers*

I don't remember the exact page—
only the look in my father's eyes when he spoke of it.

Wistful.
Shining.
Far away.
A little smile playing at the corners,
as if he could still see the page itself…
or perhaps, the wonder it once gave him.

He called it The Book of Medicine.
He said it came from Louis V—twelve
great volumes, each one a world.
Not just charts or facts or drawings, but treasures.

"See that frog?" he would say by the pond,
"That salamander? That leaf?"
"We know what we know because of Louis V—
and the Book of Medicine."

He made it sound like Eden bound in leather,
a garden you could open with your hands.

And I believed him.
Because he didn't speak of
knowledge as possession—
but as invitation.
The kind you receive with wide
eyes and a quiet breath.

To him, the world was a manuscript—
and God had written it in birdsong,
moss, and movement.

I used to think my father was
marveling at the men who made the pages.
Now I know—he was marveling
at the Author who made them.

"If men can do this," he'd say, eyes wide, voice quiet,
"just imagine what God can do—through you,
through anyone—if we'd only listen."

Not with noise.
Not with hurry.
But with the silence that listens…
the solitude that sees.

"God is always speaking," he'd add
with a knowing grin,
"but most folks are too busy making
a racket to hear Him."

And he'd chuckle,
as if to say,
"The miracle's right there.
You just missed it."

Sometimes I'd throw out
question after question—
trying to catch the wonder, trying to
name what I didn't yet know.

And he'd just smile,
tilt his head,
and say it softly,
"You're making a racket again."

It was never scolding.
It was invitation.

An invitation to stop chasing... and start listening.
To see what silence could say.

So I'd quiet down.
One eye on the pond or tree or stone—
and one eye on his face.
Watching how he watched.
Trying to guess what he was noticing...
and hoping, somehow, I'd begin to see it too.

Because I wasn't just learning the world.
I was learning how to wonder.

And now, when I pause in silence,
I swear I still see him—
watching, noticing,
waiting for me to catch the wonder too.

## *The Watchers Who Remembered*

They didn't just study the world.
They watched it like a lover listens to a heartbeat.
They didn't just read facts.

They walked with them—
let them echo in silence,
turned them over like stones,
warm from the sun.

Every frog's pulse,
every leaf's curl,
every feather's tilt in the wind—
it wasn't just seen; it was absorbed.

Leonardo sketched not to
remember, but to become.
The old physicians didn't jot notes
to publish, but to wonder—
to give thanks,
to whisper what they saw
back to the Author.

They remembered because they beheld.
They held because they slowed down.
And knowledge became part of them.

Not stored in a file.
Not tucked in a drawer.
But woven—into eye, hand,
breath, and pause.
We call them geniuses.

But maybe they were just better watchers.
Better listeners.
And maybe what they saw is still whispering—
if we'll become quiet enough to see it too.

## *Reflection:*

This seed he planted—that
wonder requires silence and seeing
requires stillness—would grow
into my understanding that
knowledge isn't just information
to be gathered, but invitation to be received.
He taught me that we are all
called to be watchers, listeners,
beholders of the sacred text written
in every leaf and stone and breath.

# SUMMER

# CHAPTER 10

# Giuseppe and the Geraniums

As summer bloomed around me, the tenth seed my father planted revealed itself through a memory of red geraniums and morning rituals. This was a lesson about courage—the kind that reaches across balconies and language barriers, trusting that kindness needs no translation.

When we moved to Italy, I was small. To me, it was the greatest of adventures.

We lived in a tall apartment building where red geraniums spilled from nearly every windowsill. The floors inside were marble—cool and smooth—and perfect for sliding across in socks. I remember the echo of laughter, the scent of fresh bread in the mornings, and the feeling that the whole world had suddenly opened up around me.

Within days, I discovered a man who would change everything.

He was old and sat every morning on the balcony directly across from ours. I suppose I was too young to realize he didn't speak English.

I didn't care.

I was up early, always, and so was he. I'd run outside and chatter away, delighted to have a new friend. He never seemed bothered—just smiled wide, nodding and laughing at my endless stories.

It's funny—I was terribly shy when people were up close, especially in crowded family gatherings or when we were traveling. I would hide behind my father's legs, overwhelmed by faces and voices.

But put a little distance between us, like the space between our balconies, and I could chatter away fearlessly.

Something about that safe space across the courtyard made me brave. Giuseppe seemed to understand this instinctively, never trying to come closer, just meeting me exactly where I felt comfortable.

Soon, our mornings turned into a ritual.

He would raise one finger as if to say, "Wait!" Then he'd reach down beside his chair and pull up an object—always something new: a flower, a fruit, a book, a spoon. He'd hold it up like a magician revealing a treasure.

Then he would say a word. One rich, delicious-sounding word in Italian.

Next, he'd point to his chest and say another word. Then point to me, eyebrows raised, inviting: "And you?"

I caught on fast.

I'd shout my name, bouncing on my toes with excitement. He'd laugh, then repeat the magical word, point to the object, then to his mouth, then to me again.

"What do you call it?" he was asking.

And just like that, I began learning Italian.

Every day brought a new word. A new connection. A new way of seeing.

I couldn't wait to show my father the game.

One morning, I dragged him out to the balcony and introduced him to my friend. My dad was enthralled. He took my hand, and together we walked across to the other building to meet the man in person.

His name was Giuseppe.

Giuseppe beamed when my father thanked him in Italian! From then on, Giuseppe became a kind of secret tutor for me. He taught me the names of flowers in the gardens, the vegetables at the market, and the stars we pointed to at night.

I was the first in our family to speak Italian fluently.

Shopping had been an incredible challenge for my mother at first. She would line us all up along the wall of the market and wait. She'd listen carefully as other customers spoke to the shopkeepers, memorizing the Italian words they used. After they left, she would approach the counter to ask for that one item.

Over and over, item by item, day after day, she slowly built her vocabulary through pure determination and patience.

But once I began learning from Giuseppe, everything changed.

Shopping became a joy instead of a trial. I walked beside her proudly, helping her ask for what she needed with confidence.

No longer waiting by the wall for someone else to speak first—we could just speak.

It was magic. All of it. And it started with a geranium. And a kind old man who saw wonder in a child and gave her the gift of language one beautiful word at a time.

I didn't understand then that my father's belief that "strangers are just friends you haven't met yet" had prepared me for Giuseppe. He had already planted the seed of openness that made me brave enough to chatter fearlessly across that courtyard.

## *Reflection*

*The Language of Welcome*

Looking back, I can see how my father often said, "Strangers are just friends you haven't met yet."

And I believed him.

So when I met Giuseppe, I didn't hesitate.

I was learning to be brave—to speak before I understood, to listen with more than just my ears, to trust that kindness needs no translation.

Sometimes, the greatest lessons don't begin with books, but with balconies, and smiles, and red geraniums waving in the breeze.

Giuseppe taught me words. But my father taught me how to walk into the world with openness—how to assume the best, to welcome the unknown, and to remember that learning begins with love.

What I came to understand was that the most profound lessons often happen not in classrooms, but in the spaces between us—across courtyards, over market counters, in the patient repetition of beautiful sounds.

This seed he planted—that learning begins with love and courage comes from connection—would grow into my understanding that language is just one way we reach toward each other.

The deeper language is the one Giuseppe and I spoke from the very first morning:
the language of welcome, of curiosity, of making room for wonder.

That's the kind of bravery I want to carry still:
the kind that makes room, that doesn't fear different sounds or faces,
the kind that says—
"Here I am. Would you like to play?"

# CHAPTER 11

# Don't Do Anything in a Hurry

In the fullness of summer, the eleventh seed my father planted began to bloom in my understanding. This was a lesson about presence—the art of moving through life with purpose but never with panic, finding wonder in the work itself rather than rushing toward its completion.

My father was never slow. Yet he was never in a rush.

He worked hard and long, but with an ease that seemed like a musical rhythm—as if he alone knew the tune that made everything flow.

Methodical, yet smooth.

He often would remind me:

"Don't be in such a rush. There's no fire! Rushing opens the door for error. Take your time. Think. It keeps you calm, and those around you calm. Then everybody stays safe and happy."

And yet, I rush.

There's always so much to get back to—exploring, reading, doing.

But he worked as if everything he did was a wonder for being done the first time.

Never mind it was likely the millionth time he had chopped wood or planted a garden or mowed a lawn.

"Boy, doesn't that grass smell lovely? Look how green it is. How does it get just that exact color that makes the green of the trees blend so beautifully?"

All the while, we children were rushing—eager to get back to riding bikes or making mud pies or swinging from vines.

And yet... the wonder is what I remember.

He never rushed because he found wonder in everything.

Watching us play. Watching us grow. Colors. Sound. Another day to be alive.

He loved life. And all its many varieties. And he was never in a hurry to rush past it or through it.

I didn't understand then that he wasn't just teaching me about time management—he was modeling a way of being. A way of moving through the world that honored both the work and the wonder.

## Reflection

*The Gift of Not Rushing*

Looking back, I can see how most of us move through life as if we're trying to catch up to something we can't name.

We rush through meals, conversations, even beauty—afraid we'll miss out on the next thing without ever fully receiving the one we're in.

But there are people—rare ones—who carry time differently. Who know how to stretch a moment like bread in the wilderness enough to feed everyone present.

My father was one of those people.

He moved through life with purpose, but never with panic.

He didn't measure success by how fast he finished a task, but by how present he remained inside it.

And without saying so, he taught me this: that wonder and gratitude live just beneath the surface—but only if you're still enough to notice.

What I came to understand was that this is one of the lessons I didn't know I was learning until years later when I realized I remembered the smell of grass more than the game I was rushing to get back to.

This seed he planted—that wonder and gratitude live just beneath the surface—would grow into my understanding that presence is a choice. Every moment offers the opportunity to rush through or to receive fully. He taught me that the quality of our attention determines the quality of our experience.

The work itself becomes sacred when we approach it with his kind of unhurried wonder.

# CHAPTER 12

# The Secret Lesson of Floating

In the warmth of summer, the twelfth seed my father planted revealed itself beside still waters. This was a lesson about floating—about finding peace on the surface even when storms rage above or currents churn below.

My father loved nature, and he passed that love on to all of us.

When my anxiety would rise—when the world felt too loud or my heart too unsettled—he would take my hand and lead me to the water's edge:

a lake,
a pond,
any place where life slowed and the world grew still.

We would sit quietly on the bank, watching the ducks together.

He would ask,
"What do you see?
Describe what the ducks are doing.
How do they look as they move?"

I would study them:
the way they glided across the water,
their bodies serene,
their feathers unruffled,
their heads bobbing gently as if in time with a secret song.

After a while, he would smile and say,
"We can learn a big lesson from these ducklings.
See how they glide?
Don't they look so happy?"

Over time, he taught me to notice more:

Whether the lake was calm or stormy,
whether the wind was gentle or wild,
whether the sky was cloudy or bright with sunlight—
the little ducks always glided along,
happy and graceful just the same.

He told me,
"Underneath the water, their feet are sometimes paddling frantically,
and sometimes they are still.
Sometimes, there's turmoil beneath the surface,
or storms above.
But the ducklings remain the same on top.
They've learned the secret lesson of floating.
It's not their job to change the weather,
or the bottom of the lake,
or even the other fowl around them.
Their job is simply to float—
and they are happy because they've learned that secret."

Life, he said, was like that.
"We all need to learn how to just float."

Once I understood, it became our quiet code.

Whenever I was ruffled by something in my day,
when worry threatened to pull me under,
he would simply say,
"Be like the ducks. Just float."

I didn't fully understand then that this simple phrase would become
one of the most practical gifts he ever gave me.
I am still learning to master this simple lesson.
I am not as adept at it yet.

He, though—
he was a master of it.

## *Reflection*

Looking back, I can see how this lesson shaped not just my approach to
anxiety, but my entire understanding of resilience.

Now, even in his absence,
when life feels stormy
or the waters beneath me churn,
I remember the ducks.

I hear his gentle voice:
"Be like the ducks. Just float."

And for a moment,
I find peace on the surface,
trusting that I, too, can learn the secret of floating.

What I came to realize was that he wasn't teaching me to be passive or
to ignore life's challenges.

He was teaching me the difference between what I could control and
what I needed to simply navigate with grace.

This seed he planted—
that we can learn to float through life's storms—
would grow into my understanding that peace isn't the absence of
turmoil,
but the ability to remain steady in the midst of it.

He taught me that like the ducks,
our job isn't to control the weather or change the depths,
but simply to trust our ability to stay afloat.

The secret lesson of floating:
sometimes the most profound strength
is found not in fighting the current,
but in learning to rest upon it.

# CHAPTER 13

# Elastic Dream Machine

In the height of summer, the thirteenth seed my father planted revealed itself through his gift for distilling wisdom into unforgettable phrases. This was a lesson about holding space—for questions without answers, for love that stretches reality, for the beautiful tension between logic and wonder.

My father had a way of saying things that stuck.

He didn't labor over words. He didn't need to. Somehow, he could speak a phrase with such clarity, such effortless truth, that it would lodge in your memory for years.

What would take me pages to explain, he could distill into a single line.

It was like magic.

He used to say that every child's first word was "Dada," but that mine was "Why?" He said I was born with a heart bigger than myself—and an endless supply of questions to match.

Whenever I'd get worked up about injustice or circular reasoning or anything that simply made no sense, I'd go on and on trying to untangle it. He'd listen quietly, then tap his forehead and say:

"Don't let logic interfere."

That was it. Nothing more. And somehow, it said everything.

He had a way of reminding me to let go of the need to make sense of what could not be made sense of. Of what couldn't be controlled, explained, or fixed.

That phrase became a kind of shorthand for peace between us.

He used it often—not to dismiss my thoughts, but to soothe my overworked mind.

Other times, he'd offer wisdom cloaked in a made-up phrase, drawn from the mysterious place in him where poetry and playfulness converged.

One of my favorite examples of this came from a letter we exchanged.

I had sent him a video of a speech by a general—someone I thought was the same man he had told stories about from his own younger days. It turned out I was wrong. It wasn't the same man at all.

But the speech had been so powerful, so inspiring, that I didn't want to just admit my mistake and move on. Instead, I found myself doubling down, expressing the kind of reverence I felt for my father every day.

To me, he was every bit as worthy of honor as any decorated general— even if the world didn't know his name.

So I wrote back:
"You're MY General Mattis."

His reply?
"That's a stretch of your elastic dream machine, but I love you for it."
—Dad

It was so perfectly him. He couldn't accept praise without deflecting first—that was his humble nature. But he always followed the deflection with love, letting me know he treasured my heart even when he couldn't quite accept my words.

"Elastic dream machine" became his gentle way of saying:

'Your love is stretching reality a bit, but I see your heart, and I love you for seeing me this way.'

That's who he was. Wise. Whimsical.

Able to hold space for the stretch between what was real and what was imagined, and love me right there in the middle of it.

I didn't understand then that both phrases—'Don't let logic interfere' and 'elastic dream machine'—were teaching me the same essential truth:
that love doesn't always need to make perfect sense to be perfectly real.

## *Reflection*

Looking back, I can see how sometimes the deepest truths come in phrases that don't exist anywhere else but in the heart of the person who spoke them.

Elastic dream machine—it sounds absurd, and yet somehow it captures everything:
imagination, longing, stretch, hope.

The desire to make sense of the world through the stories we tell, even if they bend the truth a little just to reach the heart.

What I came to realize was that my father gave me permission to stretch—to dream, to question, to play with words and truth and wonder.

And always, always, love me right there in the middle of it.

This seed he planted—that we can hold space for the stretch between what is and what we dream—would grow into my understanding that the most profound truths often live in paradox.

He taught me that wisdom isn't about having all the answers, but about being comfortable with the questions.

That love doesn't require logic to be valid.

In his elastic dream machine world, contradictions could coexist beautifully.

A shy vowel could walk beside a brave one.
A humble man could be worthy of a general's honor.
A daughter's love could stretch reality just enough to touch the truth of a father's worth.

And all of it—every beautiful, illogical, perfectly imperfect bit of it—was held together by love.

# CHAPTER 14

# The Twelfth of Never

As summer reached its peak, the fourteenth seed my father planted revealed itself through rhythm and grace. This was a lesson about harmony—how to move through life and relationships with the kind of balance that comes from hearts beating as one.

He always made maneuvering through life and people and situations look so breezy.

Like a gliding dance with my mom to the Twelfth of Never.
I could never figure out how he made it look so easy.
They didn't just dance—they floated.

That was their song. That was them. I loved watching them dance, but it always felt like eavesdropping on something sacred.

Even other dancers would stop to watch.
The way they moved, the way they looked at each other—it was spellbinding.

Cinderella and her fairy godmother had nothing on them.
It wasn't about perfect steps or polished moves. It was something else.
A kind of knowing. A secret rhythm you couldn't fake.

I would ask them endlessly,
"How do you dance like that? Did you take lessons or something?"

They'd laugh—one of those long, shared laughs that felt like home.
And then my dad would grow quiet and say,

"You can't dance with someone who doesn't know your heart. Your
hearts have to beat as one. Then the feet just follow the rhythm.

Just like a duck floats."
It never made much sense to me then.

I danced with my dad too—but not like that. Still, we knew each
other's hearts. Maybe that's what he meant. I'd keep asking questions,
and he and Mom would just share that look—the one I'd seen on the
dance floor.

And they'd say, "One day, you'll dance with a heart meant only for
you."

I didn't understand then that he wasn't just talking about dancing—he
was describing a way of being in the world.
I think about that often—how he glided through life.

Calm. Funny. Observant.

He had this way of reading a room without ever needing to dominate
it. He'd catch the undercurrents of emotion and gently steer things in a
better direction—like someone guiding a raft through a narrow bend in
the river.

He did the same with us.

I was always scribbling into one of those black-and-white speckled notebooks, narrating my world like it was a novel. One day, he came home and surprised me with my first Big 5 notebook. (Do they even make those anymore? They were the Cadillac of composition books!)

I was ecstatic. It felt like a writer's rite of passage.
My little brother, however, was upset—he hadn't gotten anything.
Without missing a beat, my dad said,

"Well, I can't have her talking my ear off all day when chores need doing!"

Then he winked at me over my brother's head to let me know he didn't mean it that way.

The very next day, my brothers each got silly putty. Balance restored. Peace brokered. No drama, no lecture—just grace in motion.

He glided through life the way he danced—with humor, with balance, with a heart that beat in rhythm with the ones he loved.


## Reflection

Looking back, I can see how he wasn't just talking about dancing—he was describing a way of being in the world.

A way of moving through relationships and situations with such grace that it looked effortless, even though it required deep attunement to the hearts around him.

Now I understand what he meant about hearts beating as one. It wasn't just about dancing—it was about how he moved through every relationship, every situation, every moment of his life.

He knew the secret rhythm of love:
how to read what others needed,
how to restore balance without creating drama,
how to glide through life's complexities with grace.

What I came to realize was that whether we're dancing or navigating
family dynamics or moving through life's complexities, the secret is the
same:
listen for the rhythm of love and let everything else follow.

This seed he planted—that true harmony comes from hearts beating as
one—would grow into my understanding that grace isn't about perfect
steps, but about perfect attention.

He taught me that the most beautiful dance isn't performed on a floor,
but lived in the everyday moments where we choose to move in rhythm
with the hearts we love.

And maybe that's what he was really teaching me—not just how to
dance, but how to live in harmony with the hearts around me.

# CHAPTER 15

# You're Only Somewhere
# You Haven't Been Yet

As summer continued to unfold, the fifteenth seed my father planted revealed itself on winding roads to nowhere in particular. This was a lesson about presence—about finding beauty in the journey itself and trusting that even when we don't know where we're going, we're still exactly where we need to be.

Long drives meandering nowhere in particular, simply to enjoy scenery and share conversation, were something my father loved doing.

He had an eagle eye that noticed things many would overlook—the color of a front door. He would remark, "I wonder what they're trying to say to us? It sure is pretty."

And if someone was outside, he'd say, "We should thank them for making it so pretty."

He noticed flowers and trees, the curve of a road, the perfect place for a picnic, a roadside farm stand where we might lend a helping hand.

I would worry.

"What if we get lost? Do we have enough gas?"

He would say, "Relax. Just enjoy the ride. There's no such thing as lost. You're only somewhere you haven't been yet. And with every tire roll you're somewhere, so you're not lost. You see the sun? Find your direction and trust it."

He was always so calm and cool and collected.

I didn't understand then that he wasn't just talking about driving—he was teaching me a way of moving through life without the anxiety of needing to control every outcome.

## Reflection

*The Roads Between*

Looking back, I can see how some people drive to get somewhere.

He drove to be somewhere—
right there with you.

Present. Curious. Listening to the land.

He saw things others missed—
not just in the scenery,
but in people,
in color,
in silence.

He reminded us that beauty is often quiet.
That noticing is a form of love.

That a journey with no destination
may take you exactly where you needed to go.

When I feared getting lost,
he never did.

He trusted the sun, the tires, the road—
and something deeper:
the truth that even when we don't know where we are,
we are still on the way.

His calm didn't come from knowing everything.
It came from knowing enough.
Enough to breathe.

To smile at a red door.
To wave at a stranger.
To say thank you to beauty.
To stop for peaches.
To take the long way home
because the long way was the gift.

What I came to realize was that the journey itself is the gift, and that
trust in the process can transform anxiety into wonder.

This seed he planted—that we're never truly lost, only somewhere we
haven't been yet—would grow into my understanding that presence is
more valuable than destination. He taught me that life's most beautiful
discoveries often happen not when we're rushing toward a goal, but
when we're open to wherever the road might lead.

The wisdom of wandering: sometimes the best way to find yourself is
to stop worrying about where you're going and start noticing where you
are.

# CHAPTER 16

# He Built Us a Hill

As summer began to wane, the sixteenth seed my father planted revealed itself in a memory of Minnesota snow and impossible dreams made real. This was a lesson about love in action—about seeing what's missing and choosing to create it rather than accept its absence.

When I was small, my father's work moved us to Minnesota. As winter approached, he grew a little sad.

There were no hills in our flat neighborhood—no slopes to sled down or snowy adventures to be had.

So what did he do?

What any loving father might dream to do—though few would follow through.

He built us a hill.

The neighbors looked on curiously. It was Minnesota, after all—snow was everywhere, but sledding hills weren't. Especially not hand-built ones.

He brought in load after load of dirt, sculpting it carefully, smoothing it, tamping it down until he got it just right.

It wasn't a huge hill—probably no more than six feet high. But we were little, and to us it was enormous. A mountain of possibility right there in our front yard.

Then he waited, grinning like a Cheshire cat, for the snow.

When it finally arrived, he bundled us up in warm coats and mittens, handed us new sleds, and ran outside with the kind of excitement only a child—or a child-hearted father—could understand.

We flew down our very own sledding hill, laughing and whooping as the snow sprayed up around us.

Soon, curious neighbors came by to join in. Mothers brought Thermoses of hot cocoa and trays of cookies. Kids built snowmen and snow forts. There were snow angels, snowball fights, and a neighborhood transformed.

Winter had turned into a wonderland—right there in our front yard.

And all because our dad thought we should have a hill.

We were overjoyed. And proud.

"That's my dad!" we said, over and over again.

I didn't understand then that he wasn't just building us a hill—he was teaching us that love doesn't just accept limitations. Love actively works to create possibilities.

# *Reflection*

*The Gift of Elevation*

Looking back, I can see how some build monuments.
Others build legacies.

He built us a hill.

Not for recognition,
but for delight—
the kind of delight that makes a child
laugh until their cheeks are red
and their scarf comes loose
from rolling in joy.

He saw what wasn't there
and decided to make it be.

That is what love does.
It moves dirt.
It shapes earth.
It elevates the ordinary
so joy can come sliding in.

What I came to realize was that when we see what's missing in someone's life, we have a choice: we can accept the absence, or we can pick up a shovel and start building.

This seed he planted—that love moves dirt to create joy—would grow into my understanding that the most profound acts of love are often the most practical ones. He taught me that love isn't just a feeling—it's a force that actively shapes the world, one shovelful at a time.

And sometimes,
if you're lucky,
the hill becomes more than just a mound of snow—
it becomes a memory that never melts.

# CHAPTER 17

# The Worry Shrub

As summer drew toward its close, the seventeenth seed my father planted revealed itself in a story about boundaries and sacred spaces.

This was a lesson about intentional presence—
about choosing what we carry into the places and relationships we hold most dear.

In the years before he died, someone once asked my father how he managed to create such a beautiful, close-knit family while being so busy with work and life.

He paused,
and then his eyes began to twinkle with that familiar spark of mischief and wisdom.

"Well," he said, "I'll tell you—and you can see if it works for you!"

He explained that just outside our doorway grew a beautiful shrub he had planted himself.

Every evening, before stepping inside, he would pause at that shrub.

He'd take a few minutes to think over his day, and then—
one by one—
he would whisper each worry,
frustration,
or lingering thought into the branches,
hanging them there like ornaments.

Only then, with his heart lightened and his mind clear, would he step
through the door to greet his family.

He wouldn't enter the house until he was sure he'd left all his worries
outside,
nestled safely in the shrub's branches.

Looking back, I can see how I remember that shrub—how it stood
faithfully by our door, never knowing it was our family's silent
guardian.

Sometimes I would watch Dad pause there in the evening light, and I
wondered what he was thinking about.

Now I know he was carefully hanging up his day so he could fully enter
ours.
"In the morning," he said, "I'd stop again,
pick them off one by one,
and begin the process all over again.
Day after day."

He grinned. "So, it worked for me. Maybe it'll work for you, too.
Now that I think of it, I believe I am remiss in never properly thanking
that shrub for holding all that for me all those years."

I didn't understand then that he wasn't just talking about managing stress—
he was teaching us about the sacred responsibility of protecting the peace of those we love.

## *Reflection*

What I came to realize was that his story always made us laugh, but it carried a lesson as deep as any he ever taught:

That we can choose where to lay down our burdens,
that home can be a place of peace,
and that sometimes the simplest rituals—rooted in nature and imagination—can help us carry on with lightness and love.

Now, whenever I see a shrub outside a doorway, I remember my father's twinkling eyes and his quiet ritual of letting go.

And I find myself silently thanking the trees and shrubs that stand sentinel,
holding space for all the worries we need to set down before we step into the warmth of home.

This seed he planted—that we can choose where to lay down our burdens—would grow into my understanding that love requires boundaries.

He taught me that home isn't just a place we enter,
but a sanctuary we actively create by being intentional about what we bring inside.

The worry shrub:
a simple reminder that sometimes the most profound acts of love
happen in the pause before we enter,
in the choice to leave our troubles at the threshold
so we can offer our families the gift of our full presence.

# CHAPTER 18

# The Acid Rain Story

As summer moved toward autumn, the eighteenth seed my father planted revealed itself in a moment of manufactured terror.

This was a lesson about discernment—
about holding fear up to the light of observable truth and choosing wonder over worry.

It was a terrifying time, I thought.
Even eating candy had become scary.

What was in it?
Stamps? Could you lick them—or were they poisoned?
The air?
The rain?

It was surreal. And it amazes me still that no one seems to remember we grew up like this.

At school, we watched filmstrips we didn't understand but couldn't forget:
atomic bombs,
angel dust,
acid rain.

No warning to parents.
No context.

Just fear downloaded into our little bodies like software we didn't ask for.

My parents were as caught off guard as we were. They hadn't known what was coming—and so couldn't prepare for our questions, our nightmares, our sudden panic over things like the sky.

We used to love when it rained.

Because when it rained, my father would grin and shout, "Oh boy! Puddles, kids! Puddles!"

And we'd race outside with him,
laughing,
stomping,
soaking in the joy.

But then one day, we burst back inside in terror.

We couldn't explain it at first. We just needed the water off—we were convinced it was burning us.

Eating our skin.
Poisoning our clothes.
Destroying the earth.
My father was stunned.
And heartbroken.

It took time for him to calm us down—to gently coax the fear out of our chests so we could name what we'd been told.

Acid rain.

So he took us to the window. He pointed to the trees. The flowers. The grass. The birds fluttering and singing, alive and well.

And he asked, quietly: "Would I ever let you play in water that would hurt you?"

Then came the deeper teaching.
Not with anger.
Not with sarcasm.

But with that thoughtful, musical cadence only he carried.

"Sometimes, experts are simply people who've learned a lot about nothing in particular."

He spoke about how easy it is to panic when you isolate one thing out of the whole.

"Knowledge is like that," he said.

"You cannot separate one particular part of something and learn much—because it is part of a whole. You must understand it in its context….

The whole."

That moment has never left me.

Not just because he calmed our fear—but because he taught us to see again.

To think.
To hold fear up to the light and ask,
What is true?

I didn't understand then that he wasn't just calming our immediate
fear—he was teaching us a way of thinking that would serve us for life.

A way of testing what we're told against what we can observe.

I think of Halloween nights
when we had to take our candy
to the police station for
inspection before we could eat it.

Any homemade treats or
fruit were automatically thrown away
- considered too dangerous to risk.

I remember an elderly woman
in our town who couldn't afford
bags of store-bought candy,
so she spent days making colored popcorn
balls for all the neighborhood children.

She was always so excited to
hand them out. But the police would
throw them away every time,
no matter how we tried to explain
that we knew her, that she was just a sweet
old lady sharing what she could afford to give.

There was also an old man who
picked apples from his own trees to share

with trick-or-treaters.
He stopped doing it when he
realized we weren't allowed to keep
them - his heart broken by seeing
his generous gifts discarded as potential threats.

Even as a child, I felt the wrongness of it -
all that time, effort, and love being
wasted because fear had taught us to
distrust the very community connections
that actually kept us safe.

## *Reflection*

*Wisdom in the Rain*

Looking back, I find myself asking: What do we give our children
when the world gives them fear?

My father gave us context.
Calm.
Truth without panic.
Wonder without denial.

He didn't dismiss our fear—he reoriented it.

He returned us to the window and let the world speak again. Let the
rain fall on leaves that did not wither. Let joy re-enter our bodies.

There is a kind of wisdom that doesn't rush to argue, but leads you
gently through the fog until you find your footing again.

He showed us that not everything you're told is truth—even if it's
dressed up like science or spoken by a voice of authority.

Truth, he said, lives inside a larger story.

And if you don't see the whole, you may miss what matters most.

Or the puddles you were made to dance in.

Decades later, I watch my daughters,
beautiful and grounded, raising
their young children with a calmness
that awes me. I see in them something
I had to consciously cultivate:
the ability to parent without that
background hum of vigilance -
without constantly scanning for the
mysterious horror that might
be lurking just out of sight.

They approach motherhood with a
mental freedom I worked to develop,
unencumbered by the generational
conditioning that kept part of my
awareness always alert for unseen dangers.

Even now, I still break apart candy
bars to check for razor blades
before eating them - a habit so
unconscious I barely notice it.

I would never give my children candy
without checking, though

I'd never tell them why.
But watching my daughters,
I realize it doesn't even occur to
them to check candy at all.
They approach simple pleasures with
a trust I had to work to cultivate.

This small difference reveals
something profound: I absorbed
certain cultural anxieties so they
could inherit confidence.
My background vigilance created
space for their spontaneity.
Two different expressions of the
same protective love.

It's in observing them that I recognize how deeply those old fears
embedded themselves in my own generation.

How we sometimes held too tightly.
Worried too loudly.

Prepared for tragedies that never came but left a shadow anyway.

And still, even among the sorrows and fragmentation of our time,
something sacred is being restored.

I am proud—so proud—of the beautiful things we have learned
amongst the horrors.

That children should not carry the weight of the world.
That preparing for darkness is not the same as living in light.

And that wonder, joy, and safety belong in every childhood.

This seed he planted—that truth lives inside a larger story—would grow into my understanding that wisdom means seeing the whole, not just the isolated parts that generate fear.

He taught me that when the world offers children terror, we can offer them context, calm, and the courage to think for themselves.

The gift of discernment:
teaching children to hold fear up to the light of observable truth,
and choose wonder over worry,
puddles over panic.

# CHAPTER 19

# The Gaze

As autumn deepened around me, the nineteenth seed my father planted revealed itself in a moment when childhood fears gave way to deeper questions about suffering and justice.

This was a lesson about the sacred responsibility of witness—

about looking suffering in the face and choosing to honor rather than turn away.

The scary filmstrips in school during the late 70s and 80s didn't just frighten us about acid rain, there were others too.

Atomic bombs and angel dust.

We practiced hiding under desks just in case…
Well, if we were preparing, it must mean something was coming, right?

I would come home with questions my parents couldn't always answer.

"What film? What dust?"

I would often ask my father, "What would we do? How will we be safe?"

He walked on water for me, so I knew I was safe if he was safe.

But what if he got hurt?
My fears mounted.

We were stacking wood together that day when I asked these hard questions.

"How do I find food? Water? Shelter?"

He would say, "You know more than you realize, and we cannot live worrying about things that may never happen. We have much to be grateful for."

"Yes, but what about people who don't live safely like we do?" I pressed.

"What do they do? How do we help them? It isn't fair. It isn't right. Now what do we do?"

He was wearing that red and black checkered jacket I loved on him. He made that little sound - 'nttss' - the one he always made when he had to say something that made him sad, or that he wished he didn't have to think about.

That gentle sound that meant he was figuring out how to carry hard truth with love.

He got very quiet and looked up from the wood pile with this faraway stare.

It felt like even the birds stopped singing.
I saw the muscle in his jaw wiggle.
His eyes got shiny.

And in a slow voice he said:

"Be grateful you do not know what it is to truly ask the questions many face every day.
Do your best to help where you can.
And never look away from anyone else's suffering.
Honor them."

I didn't understand then that he wasn't just answering my questions about safety—he was teaching me that true safety comes not from avoiding hard truths, but from having the courage to face them with love.

## Reflection

*The Gaze That Stays*

Looking back, I can see how there are moments in a child's life when a parent says something that doesn't just answer a question—it marks the soul.

That day, my father didn't give me safety.
He gave me sight.

To look suffering in the face and not look away.
To gaze—steadily, reverently—at what others endure.
To dignify their pain by not turning aside.

His eyes that day said more than words.

They said:
You are strong enough to see.
You are tender enough to care.

And both are needed.

What I came to realize was that the world tries to teach us to self-protect, to avoid what's uncomfortable, to numb ourselves to the ache of others.

But my father taught me otherwise.

Not to be consumed.
But to remain.
To see.
To honor.
The gaze we carry is a form of love.

And sometimes, it's the only shelter someone has.

This seed he planted—that we must never look away from suffering—would grow into my understanding that witness is a form of love.

He taught me that the gaze we carry can be shelter for those who suffer, and that honoring someone's pain by truly seeing it is sometimes the most sacred gift we can offer.

The sacred responsibility of witness:
to look suffering in the face with steady, reverent eyes,
and to let our gaze become a form of shelter for those who need to be seen.

# FALL

# CHAPTER 20

# Hiding in Plain Sight

As autumn arrived, the twentieth seed my father planted revealed itself through his mastery of invisible guidance.

This was a lesson about presence and perception—

about how the most profound teaching happens not through force, but through patient observation and the art of letting children discover truth for themselves.

My father had a remarkable gift:
the art of guidance without control, and protection without smothering. He seemed to dance through parenting with a kind of invisible choreography, steering us without ever seeming to push.

One time, he took us to a small island—I can't recall where exactly— but I'll never forget the way he kept dropping comments about the cemetery.

"Stay away from the cemetery," he'd say offhandedly, again and again, like it was some ominous place with hidden meaning.

So naturally, what do you think we did?

We spent the whole trip obsessed with the cemetery. We crept around it like little treasure hunters, convinced there must be some deep mystery waiting to be uncovered.

Maybe even pirates.
Or secrets.
Or ghosts.

Years later, we were shocked to overhear my dad telling another young parent how he used distraction to keep us safe.

He laughed and said, "I couldn't say, 'don't go there,' or they'd definitely go. So I just made it sound interesting in a mysterious way. I figured they'd focus all their attention there and leave the rest of the island alone. It worked like a charm."

We were floored.
"What?! You knew?!"
"There was nothing to find?!"

He doubled over laughing. "I thought you figured it out! You really didn't?"

"No!" we said. "We missed the whole island!"
He just waved it off with a grin: "You were safer there."

And then, looking back at the young parent, he pointed to us and said, "See? Proof. It works."

That's when he dropped the real bombshell:

"And they never even saw me watching them the whole time. I was in plain view the entire trip, keeping an eye on them at that cemetery.

Made me realize I needed to do a better job teaching them to be aware of their surroundings and observing skills."

We were stunned.
"You were WATCHING us?!"
"The whole time," he grinned. "You walked right past me at least a dozen times."

We still laugh about that. You know how, when you're young, you assume your parents are clueless? And then one day you realize—they were ten steps ahead the whole time.

I didn't understand then that he wasn't just playing games with us—he was teaching us fundamental life skills:
how to observe,
how to think critically,
and how to see beyond the obvious.


## *Maps and Monkeys*

My dad had a way of hiding in plain sight.
Not just physically—but in the way he taught.

Everywhere we went, he turned the world into a game of observation and imagination.

At the Colosseum, he'd say, "Close your eyes. Pretend none of the tourists are here. What would it smell like? What would you hear? What would the women be wearing? What food would they be eating?"

At the Leaning Tower: "Do you think it always leaned? What if it had been straight—would it be as interesting?"

Then: "Let's draw it."
He gave each of us a small notebook and encouraged us to draw our
own maps of the places we visited—not the official ones, but our own
highlights.

Whatever stood out to us—
food carts,
stray cats,
funny signs,
the color of the stones.

At the end of each day, we'd compare our maps and always decide ours
were better than the ones in the guidebooks.

One day, we'd all drawn the same thing—an old man selling roasted
chestnuts from a little cart. We children had all sketched the kind, old
man, his cart, or the warm paper cones of chestnuts.

My dad, however, had added a tiny monkey on the man's shoulder.
"A monkey?" we said. "Nice try!"
We were sure he'd added it as a playful trick, to test our attention.

But the next day, he brought us back—and there it was.
The monkey had been there all along. A real, live monkey, perched
right on the man's shoulder.

We had all missed it.
He smiled and said, "Just because you're looking, doesn't mean you're
seeing."
Looking back, I can see how that day, he taught us something we've
never forgotten: how easy it is to miss what's right in front of you.

That observation requires presence.
That sometimes, the most important things are hidden in plain sight.

## *Reflection*

What I came to realize was that my father understood something profound about learning: that the most important lessons can't be forced, only discovered.

Whether he was protecting us with a cemetery distraction or teaching us to truly see with a hidden monkey, he knew that wisdom reveals itself to those who are ready to receive it.

He was always hiding in plain sight—
his love,
his guidance,
his protection—
waiting for us to develop the eyes to see what had been there all along.

And sometimes, the cleverest teacher is the one who lets you discover the lesson when you're ready—while smiling quietly from the shadows, knowing he's already planted the seed.

This seed he planted—that wisdom reveals itself to those ready to receive it—would grow into my understanding that the best teaching doesn't announce itself.

He showed me that love, guidance, and protection are often most effective when they operate quietly, allowing children to feel independent while remaining safely watched.

The art of invisible guidance:
teaching children to see truly while protecting them completely,
all while hiding in plain sight with a smile that says,
"I've been here all along."

## CHAPTER 21

# The Pileated Woodpecker

As autumn deepened around me, the twenty-first seed my father planted revealed itself in the hammering of a rare bird.

This was a lesson about listening deeply—
about hearing not just sounds, but the stories they tell about the hidden workings of the world.

One day when I was a child, while working out back with my father, we heard a loud hammering sound echoing through the woods behind us.

It was so loud I couldn't imagine anyone hammering that hard—especially not out in the forest!

My father dashed into the house and came back out with his binoculars. He scanned the tree line, then suddenly said, "Come! It's a pileated woodpecker! Hurry!"

"A what woodpecker?" I asked, puzzled.
"Did you say a peeled woodpecker?"

We hurried into the woods, stopping now and then to listen, to look.
He told me to keep an eye out for wood chippings at the base of trees.

"Wood chippings?" I said, confused. "Like pencil shavings?"
"No," he laughed. "Much bigger. You'll see."

And sure enough—before long, we found them:
long, curled shavings scattered at the foot of a tree.

My dad pointed upward.
And there it was.
The biggest woodpecker I had ever seen.

Its head a bold streak of red, hammering so fiercely I couldn't believe it
didn't knock its head off.

My father was beaming.
"I can't believe it—we've got one right here in our woods," he said.
Then he turned serious.

"It's a good thing we heard it," he explained. "This bird is feeding on
insects that live in dead or dying trees. If it's that high up and still
finding food, it means the tree is rotting all the way through."

He looked up at the trunk thoughtfully.

"This tree will need to come down before it falls and hurts someone—
or takes a healthy tree with it."

He always said it was wise to get advice, especially when trees and living
things were at risk. So our forestry man would come and confirm.

But the woodpecker had told us first.

I didn't understand then that he wasn't just teaching me about birds—
he was teaching me to be a student of the world, to listen for the stories
that nature tells to those who know how to hear them.

Years later, on vacation in a state far from home, I heard that same deep hammering echoing across a quiet afternoon.

My uncle paused and asked, "Who on earth would be making that racket way out here?"

I grinned. "Not who. What. It's a pileated woodpecker."
He looked at me like I had just invented the name. "Are you sure that's what it's called?"

So I led him into the woods, just like my father had led me—
pausing,
listening,
scanning for chips and shapes.

And when I found it, I ran and got my dad.

Sure enough, I was right.

When my uncle realized I hadn't been making it up, I realized something else too—just how rare it was to see one of these birds.

And I felt so proud.

Proud that my dad knew something so few others did.
Proud that he had shared it with me.

And grateful that he had taught me not just to hear the hammering, but to understand what it meant—that even in the woods, there are stories being told if you know how to listen.

## *Reflection*

Looking back, I can see how my father had a gift for hearing what others missed—not just the hammering of a rare bird, but the story it was telling about hidden dangers and natural wisdom.

What I came to realize was that he taught me that the world is constantly speaking to us, offering both wonder and warnings, if we know how to listen.

That day in the woods, he gave me more than knowledge about a pileated woodpecker.

He gave me the confidence to trust what I'd learned,
the joy of sharing rare discoveries,
and the understanding that nature's most important messages often come disguised as simple sounds echoing through the trees.

This seed he planted—that the world is constantly speaking to those who know how to listen—would grow into my understanding that knowledge becomes truly valuable when we can share it with others.

He taught me that the rarest discoveries are often hidden in plain sound, waiting for someone with the patience to listen and the wisdom to understand.

The gift of deep listening:
hearing not just the hammering, but the story it tells about hidden dangers and natural wisdom,
and carrying that knowledge forward to share with others who have forgotten how to hear.

# CHAPTER 22

# The Seasons of Trees

As autumn reached its peak, the twenty-second seed my father planted revealed itself in the changing leaves around me.

This was a lesson about wholeness—
about loving not just the beautiful seasons, but embracing the entire cycle of growth, rest, renewal, and letting go.

My father was a master of observation.

Whenever we walked our land, he would ask for details—
texture,
leaf patterns,
the color of bark,
the way certain birds or animals favored particular trees.

He encouraged me to notice how each tree had its own character, and how every season brought a peculiar beauty that belonged only to itself.

He taught me to see Fall's beauty in the falling leaf—how the act of letting go created a tapestry of brilliant color and the quiet promise of new growth.

Winter's beauty, he showed me, was found in starkness. With the leaves gone, the world became a gallery of silhouettes and hidden things—
branches,
nests,
and the subtle forms that summer's fullness concealed.

Spring was a celebration:
the budding of new life,
the return of green,
and the joyful choruses of birds joining the trees in song.

Summer's beauty was in the shade cast by full, lush leaves, the gentle breeze whispering through their volumes, and the secret strength of a high limb—perfect for perching with a delicious book.

He taught me to appreciate not just one season, but the whole.

"To truly love a tree," he would say, "you must love all its seasons. The seasons are not separate, but tied together by an invisible string—each one dependent on the others, each one shaping the tree's story."

I didn't understand then that he wasn't just teaching me about trees— he was teaching me about life, about relationships, about the beauty that exists in every phase of existence.

## *Reflection*

Looking back, I can see how when I walk among the trees, I remember his questions, his careful attention, his reverence for the cycles of life.

I see that every season—of the forest, and of my own life—has its own beauty, its own lessons, its own place in the story.

To appreciate one, I must learn to appreciate them all.

And just as the trees speak and shape meaning in the world around them, so do we.

We move through seasons—
times of growth,
of fading,
of stillness,
of renewal—
and with each, we leave an imprint.

We speak into our families, we shape the world with our presence.

What I came to realize was that the people we love are not always in the same season we are.

But that is no reason to turn away.
It is a reason to look closer.

To find the beauty in their fall, their winter, their spring.
To listen not just to the season we're in—but to the season unfolding in those we meet.

This is what the trees taught my father.
This is what my father taught me.

This seed he planted—that to truly love something, you must love all its seasons—would grow into my understanding that the deepest relationships require us to find beauty in every phase.

He taught me that just as trees need winter's rest to produce spring's growth, people need all their seasons to become who they're meant to be.

And this is what I now hope to carry forward:
To walk with wonder,
to listen for seasons,
and to love the whole tree.

# CHAPTER 23

# Sentinel Trees

As autumn drew toward its close, the twenty-third seed my father
planted revealed itself in the towering trees around me.

This was a lesson about endurance—
about the difference between shallow growth that breaks under pressure
and deep roots that allow us to bend without breaking.

My father was in awe of trees.

He taught us to make maple syrup, and every spring, the sugar shack
became the heart of our world. Each night, the sweet aroma of sap
cooking filled the air, mingling with laughter and the stories my father
spun—
tales of his own childhood,
of seasons past,
of lessons learned beneath the branches
of ancient trees.

On weekends, families gathered to learn and sugar with us. The sugar
shack was alive with children playing, adults sharing stories, and
mothers preparing a feast that seemed to last all day.

I loved watching everyone work
together,
helping,
learning,
and passing on knowledge.

It was a living example of cooperation, generosity, and the joy of community.

But it was in the quiet walks through our forests that my father's reverence for trees truly came alive. He would pause beside a towering maple or a sturdy oak, his hand resting on the rough bark, and say, "Look at how this tree endures."

He taught me that the trees which survive the fiercest storms are not those that spread their roots quickly and shallowly in every direction, but those that drive their roots deep into the earth before reaching their arms to the sky.

"Deep roots hold them and ground them," he explained, "and allow them to bend with the howling winds.

The trees that spread their roots too quickly, staying close to the surface, may look strong, but they cannot bend.

When the storms come, they snap and break."

He showed me that the trees which dig deep and reach high before spreading their branches grow many healthy limbs—able to withstand the weight of snow, the force of wind, the passing of years.

"Trees with shallow roots are like spectators of the forest," he'd say.

"They're so busy reaching out to their neighbors before growing tall that their branches can't hold up under the storms."

I didn't understand then that he wasn't just teaching me about trees—he was showing me how to build a life that could weather any storm.

How to grow strong from the inside out.
My father was my sentinel tree.

He stood strong and steady, his roots deep in the soil of our family, his arms always reaching upward and outward—
sheltering,
teaching,
enduring.

Now, without him, it feels hard to breathe.
The forest feels emptier, the winds colder.

Sometimes I wonder if my own roots are deep enough to weather the storms without him beside me.

But I try to remember how he taught me to endure:
To drive my roots deep,
to reach for the sky,
and to bend when the storms come.

## *Reflection*

Looking back, I can see how I miss the house full of children, the laughter, the feasting, the stories. But most of all, I miss the quiet strength of my father—my sentinel tree.

What I came to realize was that his strength wasn't just in his presence, but in the roots he helped me establish. The deep foundations of love, wisdom, and endurance that he spent years helping me cultivate.

Now, when life feels stormy or uncertain, I walk among the trees and listen for his voice in the rustle of leaves, reminding me to root myself deeply, to reach for the light, and to endure.

This seed he planted—that deep roots allow us to bend without breaking—would grow into my understanding that true strength comes not from rigid resistance, but from flexible endurance.

He taught me that like the sentinel trees, we must root ourselves deeply in what matters most before reaching out to serve others.

The legacy of the sentinel tree:
standing strong not through rigidity, but through deep roots that allow us to bend with life's storms while never breaking, never falling, never failing to shelter those who need our strength.

# CHAPTER 24

# The Land He Gave Us

## *A Father's Quiet Legacy*

As autumn drew to its close, the twenty-fourth seed my father planted revealed itself in the very ground beneath my feet.

This was a lesson about legacy—
about how true heroism doesn't seek recognition, but quietly builds something lasting for others to inherit.

He never told us how many lives he saved.

We never knew entirely of all his medals, though they were there—quietly tucked away in drawers, not as trophies, but reminders.

He didn't come home from war looking for applause.
He came home and planted trees.

After flying rescue missions in a far-off land, after leading with calm and coming back with stories mostly unspoken, he returned to the land he had bought.

Not just for himself—
but for his parents.

For his sister.
For his children.

Many acres each.
A Christmas tree farm and wild forest.

Cousins racing through trees, collecting syrup, delighting in play,
wonder and love. Our grandparents just across the way.

I didn't understand then that he was still flying rescue missions—just
now, on the ground.

He was building something no war could tear down:
a life rooted.

A home of belonging.
But that wasn't all.

He gave part of our forest to the Boy Scouts and Eagle Scouts.

Not to clear it,
not to build cabins,
not to leave a mark on the land—
but to learn from it.

He taught them how to build a camp without destroying what gave it
shelter.

No cutting unless it had already fallen.
No scars on living bark.

A good forester, he said, uses what is given—
fallen branches,
bent limbs,

what the forest has already offered—
and leaves it as close to the way he found it as possible.

They listened.

And each year, those boys, on their way to becoming men, returned to
the woods to test their hands and hearts.

And every summer, on the final day of camp, we cooked a feast.

Our whole family carried it through the trees—balancing pots and
pies, singing ridiculous songs as we walked what seemed miles into the
hush of the forest.

We celebrated their success—not with badges or speeches, but with
cast-iron cooked chicken and potatoes, apple pie and laughter and
firelight, and the rustle of pine boughs overhearing it all.

He loved it—
watching their confidence bloom,
their respect deepen,
their joy in being part of something wild and worthy.

And then, when the fire burned low, he would take them to a clearing
beneath the stars.

There, in the open arms of the forest, he would lift his hand and
point—
Orion,
Cassiopeia,
the arc of the Milky Way.

He told the stories, ancient and sacred.

And as the boys gasped and whispered, he would smile with the kind of joy that echoes in the bones.

The timbre of his voice was like the forest itself—
deep and rooted,
ageless and alive.

Helping them see a world that was always there, but never quite like this.

What I came to realize was that his approach to the land reflected everything he'd learned about service—that true leadership means creating something that will flourish long after you're gone.

He gave them more than skills.
He gave them wonder.

A glimpse of what it means to belong to something without owning it.

He never needed to say much.
His life said it all.

We didn't know the number of missions.
We didn't know how many medals.
We only knew the way he walked the land.

Quiet.
Strong.
Humble.

Leaving behind more than he took.
Always.

This seed he planted—that legacy is built through quiet service rather than loud recognition—would grow into my understanding that the most profound heroism happens not in moments of glory, but in years of patient cultivation.

He taught me that we honor our gifts not by displaying them, but by using them to create lasting beauty for others.

The quiet hero's legacy:
transforming a warrior's heart into a gardener's hands,
creating life and wonder instead of destruction,
and teaching others to belong to something without owning it.

# CHAPTER 25

# There Is No Such Thing as Neutral

As I prepared to enter the confluence of all my father's teachings, the twenty-fifth seed he planted revealed itself with startling clarity.

This was a lesson about moral courage—
about the responsibility to witness, to remain present, and to understand that neutrality itself is a choice.

My father taught me that neutral is a lie.
"Neutral," he'd say, "is a decision. A choice."

Then he'd point to the mountain.
"Look at it. What do you see?"
"A mountain," I'd say. "It's standing."
"Is that all? Is it just being majestic? What is it doing?"

Then he'd ask again, slower, more intent:
"What is it saying?"

I'd pause. "Be tall?"
"Yes! And more. Where is it pointing?"
"Up. Forward."

He'd smile. "Exactly."
The mountain is not neutral.

It is speaking.
It is a watchman.
It stands and holds the truth.
It is a witness.
It watches and reveals.
It points the way.
It makes you look up—
and ahead.
It warns of storms before they reach you.
It testifies, simply by remaining.

"There will be times," he told me, "when you won't be able to change
things or help others the way you wish.

But you must not look away.
You must dignify what is happening.

Remain.
Witness.
Be present."

The mountain does not run.
It holds much—
and therefore, it grows tall.

Tall enough that those with eyes may see,
and those with ears may listen,
and those who seek may find their way.

# *Live*

I see the sunshine spill across the day—
    gold on green, promise in the air.
        Clouds gather at the horizon's hem,
            mountains holding their silence—
          heralds of what's to come,
            witnesses. Waiting.

A hush,
    then the soft applause of rain—
        silver threads stitching earth to sky.

I watch the wide world receive:
    meadow, field, rocky outcrop,
        each patch of ground
            opening or resisting
                in its own secret way.

Beyond the mountains,
    a bruise begins to blossom in the sky—
        deep blue, then purple,
            a greenish ache spreading wide,
          veined with yellow flashes
                as lightning fingers the horizon.

Thunder rolls,
    wind rises,
        the air turns sharp as memory.

Rain hardens into hail—
    white stones tumbling from heaven,

falling slow as thought,
quick as consequence.

I watch as the earth receives
or shatters:
soft soil yields,
lets the ice melt into blessing;
hard ground cracks,
echoes with the sound
of what it cannot hold.

Lightning carves its jagged script
across the sky—
veins of fire writing life into the dark,
splitting the crust of fallow ground.

Troughs bloom where energy met earth,
cradling rain like a mother holds her child—
each channel a womb for what will grow.

Shattered soil remembers now
how to drink, how to yield,
how to let the old, dead crust
crack open into green.

Time stirs,
rushes forward—
the storm, spent,
moves on.

Warmth returns,
the sun edges out,
gentle rain falls again,
a benediction.

I walk among the aftermath—
    pools in the low places,
        green shoots daring through broken crust,
            petals bruised but shining,
              the hush after thunder
                alive with birdsong.

A thought, like rain,
    travels from the far fields of my mind,
        seeps down, drop by drop,
            through roots and stone—
              filtered, refined—
                until it pools quietly in my heart,
                    where all that has fallen
                        is immersed in recognition.

Within this awareness,
    light and rain mingle,
        a dawning from within—
            and in that gentle brightness,

I hear it—carried in the flow of wind…
    whispering the quiet imperative
        threaded through all things:

    Live,
        Live,
            LIVE

# CHAPTER 26

# To Lasso the Moon

## *On the Range of Love*

In the confluence of all my father's teachings, I discovered the most important seed he planted—not through words, but through presence.

This was a lesson about the range of love—
about how imperfect hearts can create perfect belonging when they choose to keep showing up.

I think my father lasso'd the moon.

Not because our relationship was always perfect—but because love doesn't need perfection to last.

There were times I didn't understand why he said what he did.
Times he didn't understand me either.

But we never needed perfect understanding—because we knew each other's hearts.

And that knowing made room for difference without division,
for freedom without severing.

To cut off relationship is to say, "I truly believe you meant to hurt me."

But my father didn't wake up each morning looking for ways to wound.

He was doing what most parents do:
trying—imperfectly, beautifully—to give his children a life better than his own.

Children used to love their parents like that too.
Not because their parents were perfect—but because they were theirs.

We've forgotten how to do that.
We've been trained to believe that anything less than emotional fluency is neglect. That any unmet moment is a moral failure.

But love is not a spreadsheet.
Family is not an equation.

Parents with more than one child are not failing just because love doesn't look the same at every moment, in every direction.

What comforts one child overwhelms another.
What inspires one may silence another.

Some days, one child needs more.

That doesn't mean the others are forgotten—only that the heart is triaging with love.

It's like teaching a class. No one expects a teacher to give every student the same grade, the same sentence, the same smile, on the same day.

Why would we expect that of our parents?

It is a range.
Not all notes in a song are the same pitch—but all are needed for harmony.

Love is not about sameness.
It is about presence.

And over time, presence becomes trust.
And trust says: "You were doing your best. I see that now."

So no, my father didn't always get it right.
But he showed up.

He tried.
He gave.
He loved in the language he had.

And to me, that's as good as lassoing the moon.

## *Reflection*

*The Grace to See the Whole Symphony*

Every life is a symphony.
And no one hears it all at once.

We remember a dissonant note—a moment of silence when we needed song. We cling to a sharp word, forgetting the thousand quiet kindnesses that came before and after.

But what if we stepped back?

What if we listened not just to a measure, but to the full composition? What if we believed that even imperfect love can be real, can be formative, can be enough?

Your father may not have said the thing you needed in the exact moment you needed it. He may have missed a cue, been off rhythm, spoken in the wrong key.

But was he playing?
Did his heart strain toward your melody?
Did he try, again and again, to find harmony with you?

Then maybe you weren't unloved.

Maybe you were deeply loved by someone who was still learning how to love.

Honor doesn't mean rewriting the story—but it does mean widening the lens.

Stepping back far enough to see what your heart couldn't see at the time.

It takes humility to admit that our view has been partial.
It takes courage to believe that love was present, even when imperfectly played.

So listen again.
Not to the part that still stings, but to the pattern underneath.

The steady rhythm of showing up.
The tenderness behind the tone.
The ache of a parent who longed to give you the moon.

# CHAPTER 27

# No One Left Behind

In the confluence of all my father's teachings, one of the most challenging seeds he planted began to reveal its full meaning.

This was a lesson about the dignity of staying—

about the difference between healthy boundaries and the culture of discarding that breaks hearts and severs souls.

Boundaries are not elimination.

Healthy boundaries are never meant to annihilate relationship—unless there's true danger, and even then, it is the vulnerable who must seek shelter, not the powerful who do the cutting.

My father used to shake his head at what he called "the culture of discarding."

It broke his heart.

He saw something growing in the world—this rising trend of isolation, of estrangement, of walking away from essential relationships over things he found... small.

"They don't get me."
"They worked too much."
"They're different from me."

He was dumbfounded.
And then he'd ask:

"Did you eat every day?
Did you have a bed to sleep in?
Did you go to school, play sports, get tucked in at night?
Did someone change your diapers, wipe your tears, teach you how to tie your shoes?

Then maybe they weren't perfect. But they were your parents. And they showed up."

He never discounted hurt—but he believed that love meant more than shared opinions or personality types. He believed in honor. He believed that family and friendship are too precious to throw away.

And then, one day—after a long pause, in one of his more solemn letters—he wrote:

"Lonely is a terrible thing. But forgotten. Forgotten. That is the worst thing.
No one should be forgotten."

That was the core of him.
Yes, boundaries are sometimes necessary.

But cutting someone out of your life because they didn't fit your version of perfection?

That's something else entirely.

Because none of us are perfect.
And when you throw someone away, both of you lose.

## *Reflection*

*The Dignity of Staying*

We live in an age of exits.
Block. Delete. Unfollow. Cut ties.

All in the name of self-preservation.
But my father's wisdom whispered a deeper truth:

Dignity stays.
Dignity makes room.
Dignity asks questions before it draws lines.

He never confused boundaries with abandonment, nor protection with
punishment.

He believed most people are not trying to harm you—they're simply
human, trying to survive their own story.

And yes, sometimes love requires distance.
But distance isn't the same as dismissal.
You can guard your peace without closing the door to reconciliation.
He taught us to honor the story we do not yet understand.

To pause.
To listen for the symphony beneath the sour note.

Because no one is just one moment.

My father loved people. All people.
He welcomed them without requiring alignment, agreement, or approval.

He didn't love from strategy—he loved from the center of who he was.

No performance.
No agenda.
Just presence.

He believed that love keeps a candle in the window.
That even if someone wanders, they should still see light from home.

And above all, he believed that being forgotten is the deepest wound a soul can bear.

So we do not forget.

We remember with courage.

We love with boundaries—but also with dignity.

We stay—when we can—because sometimes presence itself is what saves the story.

# CHAPTER 28

# He Still Feeds Me

In the deepest confluence of all my father's teachings, the final seed he planted revealed itself in the smallest of creatures.

This was a lesson about continuing presence—
about how love transcends death and continues to nourish us through the mystery of offering and sacrifice.

While walking past a bush, we noticed—hidden among the feathered greenery—the tiniest of hummingbirds, face up and still. The dearest little bird, with the most delicate of beaks, lay unnoticed by the world.

As I gazed in sorrow over its tiny, lifeless form, I saw a red ant crawl across its open eye.

The sight startled me.
And in that moment, I remembered...
Not one sparrow falls to the ground without My Father knowing.

And how much more... you.
I continued to gaze—filled with wonder and astonishment.

That such a tiny bird, hidden from view... and even this smallest red ant... are seen, and known, and loved by our Creator.

And how much more…
You.
Me.

Such a powerful comfort.

Even now, when I remember that tiny hummingbird, I no longer see only its stillness. I see it in motion—alive again, joyfully flitting around me in circles of light. And the ant? Even it was provided for… life continuing through the mystery of death.

In that moment, I also remembered what my father used to tell me:

if I ever wanted to learn about life—or understand the questions I couldn't yet answer—I should pay attention to the birds and the ants. They teach by how they live, he would say.

There is much we can learn from them.
And here they were—together.

The hummingbird and the ant.
One had passed from view.
One remained—still walking in the visible realm.

And something stirred in my soul.
My father has passed on… and I am still here.

But he still feeds me.
Even now.
Even in this.

Over my shoulder, I heard a passerby
explaining to a child who had noticed the bird:

"What happened? Why did it die?"
"Survival of the fittest! I guess the red ant is stronger."

And they walked on.

How differently we see.
I saw not weakness.
Not strength.
I saw love.

That upward gaze—Creator and created, eyes once locked together.
The tiny hummingbird lying in peaceful surrender, not in defeat, but in offering.

It is not weakness, but the greatest strength, to offer whatever bit you are—however small, however overlooked—to become nourishment and sustenance for others.

I would even say—that is love.

This moment became a parable, just as my father said it could. And in the smallest of ways, I was taught again:

By the birds.
By the ants.
By the echo of a father's voice that still guides me.

He still feeds me.

# CONFLUENCE: WHERE LOVE FLOWS

# Follow the Water

We always walked the forest. Part of our property included an old road—once the main thoroughfare before the new one was laid. It wound its way through the trees in quiet and peace, lined by stone walls marking its forgotten boundaries. It felt like walking through another time.

Along the way were resting places where all sorts of things could be found—rusted buckets, pieces of old oaken barrels, fragments of green and blue glass.

My father explained that long ago, merchants and farmers, or families with heavy wagons, sometimes got stuck—bogged down in mud or snow. When they couldn't move forward, they would lighten their load, leaving behind what they could no longer carry.

It made me sad to think of it—all that time and effort, all those precious things abandoned when the journey became too difficult. But it was also magical, exploring what remained. We would imagine who these things belonged to, what their stories were, what they had to leave behind.

Even then, I was learning that sometimes we must release what we cannot carry in order to find our way home.

It was easy to lose track of time and daylight.

This is when my father would remind me:
Watch for the sun.
Feel the wind.
Notice the air.

And then he told me something I never forgot—words that would become a lifeline I didn't know I'd need.

If you're ever lost…
find water.
A stream. A river. Even just a trickle.
Follow it downstream.
It may twist and wander, but trust it.
It will always lead you to people,
to a town,
to home.

I tucked it away, like a spell. A secret I hoped I'd never have to use.

But then one day—I did.

I had been hopping from one discarded treasure to another, lost in imagination, and didn't notice how far I had wandered. The light was fading. The woods felt different.

I was beginning to panic.

And then—his voice, clear as if he were standing beside me.
Find water.

I looked around. No sun. Just shadows. But there—just a glint. A tiny stream, winding its way through roots and moss. Something in me recognized this as more than mere water—it was guidance made visible, trust given form.

I started walking quickly downstream.
It meandered.
It zigzagged.
I wondered if it would ever really lead anywhere.

It was getting dark enough to be frightening. But my father's voice whispered through my doubt: the stream doesn't need to rush or run straight—it simply knows where it's going.

Still I followed. Looking. Hoping. Remembering. Learning what it means to trust something you cannot see the end of.

And then—I looked up.
There, through the trees, I saw it:
the soft golden light from our kitchen window,
glowing like a beacon
from the back side of the house.

I was still a ways off, but I couldn't believe it.
The stream had brought me home.

I raced toward the light, stumbling over roots, heart pounding with joy and relief—and something deeper. A recognition that what had seemed like wandering had been leading all along.

Just as I burst through the back door, I collided with my father—who had been checking to see if I'd returned and was heading back out to look for me again.

He had been searching the whole time.

I jumped into his arms, yelling,
"You were right! You were right! The water brought me home!"

He laughed and hugged me, but I could feel his heart still catching up
with mine. Relief passed between us like breath.

And though we never made a big deal about it again, something
in me had changed. I had learned that trust isn't about seeing the
destination—it's about following what you know will lead you home.

I had trusted the water.
I had trusted what he taught me.
And it had led me exactly where I needed to be.

Looking back now, I realize that day was never just about getting un-
lost. It was about learning to surrender. The stream didn't run straight.
It didn't rush. It didn't even seem sure of itself. But it knew where it was
going—and more importantly, I learned to trust that it did.

That seed he planted—the wisdom to trust the water—was never really
about survival. It was about faith. About learning to follow even when
the path winds, even when fear whispers, even when you're not quite
sure if it will lead anywhere at all.

He taught me that the stream always flows toward life. Toward others.
Toward home.

And now, years later, as I near the final chapters of his story,
I find I am still following that water.
Still trusting it to carry what I cannot hold.
Still believing it will bring him Home...
and one day, me too.

# CHAPTER 29

# Heartbeat and Rosebuds

In the confluence where all love flows, I discovered the first seed my father planted—not through words or lessons, but through presence itself.

This was the foundation beneath all foundations:
the rhythm of safety,
the heartbeat of trust,
the sound before words that would shape everything that followed.

When I was a baby, I was a terrible sleeper.

My father loved it.
He said it was because he had me all to himself.

In the quiet hours before dawn, he would wake before I did and sit beside my bassinet, listening for the faintest stir. The moment I made a sound, he'd scoop me up eagerly—not groggy or begrudging, but delighted—so he could change me himself.

Then he'd carry me back to their bed, lay me on his chest, and rest my tiny head right above his heart.
There, he would whisper stories.

Of how precious I was.
Of how happy he was that we were both such poor sleepers.
Of how this sacred time belonged only to us.

With his steady heartbeat beneath my cheek and his voice humming just above it, my breathing would begin to settle. But he would force himself to stay awake—not wanting to miss a single moment of holding me close.

Sometimes my mother would stir and scold him gently, telling him I'd never learn to sleep if he kept spoiling me like this.

He would smile and say, "Look how tiny she is. Her breath is like rosebuds in bloom. She'll grow up too soon as it is. Let be."

And then he would go on spinning tales of wonder, speaking softly into my spirit when all I knew was felt.

To this day, I cannot fall asleep without a story being read aloud… and the sound of a heartbeat near.

As I grew into a toddler, these rituals had to shift. My father was at work during the day, and my mother struggled to get me to nap. But one day, she found me sprawled across our large white Labrador, Logger, like a tiny rider on a gentle horse. I had climbed up and stretched myself along his broad spine, using him as my living bed. Logger paced slowly—patiently—back and forth across the room, carrying me while I slept, my little hand reaching down along his side to rest against his steady heartbeat.

My mother was so moved by this scene that she photographed it - showing Logger's patient devotion as he served as my walking, breathing cradle.

Somehow, I had found the rhythm again.

I had found the story.
I had found the heartbeat.

And I slept.

## Reflection

*The Sound Before Words*

We are shaped long before we are taught.

Before we know what love is, we feel it.
Before we understand story, we are written into one.

My father gave me more than comfort in the dark—he gave me the rhythm of safety, the heartbeat of trust.

In those wordless hours, a foundation was laid beneath memory, beneath language, beneath time.

The voice of a father, not demanding, but delighted.
Not training me, but treasuring me.

What a strange and beautiful thing it is, that the nervous system remembers what the mind forgets—and that a baby held to a chest in the night can grow into a woman who still searches for the sound of a story and the thrum of a heart to guide her to rest.

Sometimes the greatest truths are planted before we have words to receive them.

And sometimes the way a father holds a child is the first gospel she will ever hear.

# CHAPTER 30

# Still Breathing Together

## *A Full Circle*

In the confluence where all love flows, I discovered how the first rhythm my father gave me would become the last rhythm I could give him.

This was a lesson about the cyclical nature of love—
how what begins in infancy comes full circle in the sacred act of presence during life's final season.

The sicker my father grew, his need for oxygen increased.
It comforted him not to be alone at night—especially then.

And our roles had shifted.

Now I was the one listening for his breathing in the dark.

The oxygen machine hummed—its rhythm both sustaining and haunting—a mechanical melody that both kept him alive and distanced him from the world around him.

He couldn't hear as well with the machine on, couldn't catch the soft sounds of conversation or the gentle murmur of nighttime that had always comforted him.

One evening, as he adjusted the tube with quiet frustration, he looked at me with those same eyes that once watched over my bassinet.

I knew what he was searching for.
But the machine drowned it out.
The constant whoosh and click made it
hard for him to hear my breath.

So I leaned closer and whispered,
"It's okay, Dad. Now I get to hear your breath. And I love that you're still breathing with me."

His eyes softened.
That familiar smile—the one I'd known since infancy—spread across his face.

We had come full circle.
From him treasuring my infant breath on his chest to me treasuring each breath he took beside me.

From his heartbeat lulling me to sleep to the rhythm of his oxygen machine becoming my new lullaby.

The sound was different now—mechanical instead of natural—but the love underneath was exactly the same.

Our roles had shifted.
Now I was the one listening for his breathing in the dark.

I listen..still..

## *Reflection*

*The Rhythm That Remains*

Love has its own breathing pattern.

In and out.
Give and receive.
Hold and be held.

What begins in infancy—that primal need for the sound of another's life—never really leaves us.

It just changes form.
First, I needed his heartbeat to find my rhythm.
Then, he needed mine to remember his.

The machines may hum.
The breath may labor.
But underneath the mechanical sounds,
the original song continues:

I am here.
You are here.
We are breathing together.

This is love.

Sometimes the greatest gift we can give is simply to remain present to the sound of someone's existence—to let them know that their breathing, however it comes, is still music to us.

And sometimes, if we're very lucky, we get to return the favor of being someone's favorite sound in the dark.

# Drowning and Floating

I kept vacillating—
between thinking—
I am drowning
and he is drowning.

I was drowning in the knowing,
and he was drowning in the going,
and I could not save either one of us.

The air felt like water.
Inside and out—
it wrapped around everything.

Suffocating.
Enveloping.
Melding us together
in the unrelenting stillness.

I sat.
And sat.
And sat.
Helpless.

And then, a strange thought rose—
Maybe we are floating in the drowning.

Maybe this ache
isn't the end,
but the middle.

He used to tell me to remember the ducks.

Why could I never float?
Why did I always sink,
even when the water was calm?

Now it's storming softly,
and I wonder—
Was he teaching me to float
when the world feels like drowning?

To ride the ache.
To trust the water.
To remember the ducks.

And still,
I return to the silence,
where breath was his final word
and rain fell like a whispered letting go.


## *A Bend in the River*

The silence did not end there.
It rushed in like a river—
slipping in through the window cracks,
curling around the bed,

and flowed through my veins,
filling my bones.

It echoed in my chest,
floodwaters rising,
threatening to breach the dam
I didn't know I'd built.

It kept building—
like breathing underwater,
as I watched him rushing
into rapids where I couldn't reach him,
couldn't hold on.

He had taught me about rivers—
how they always bend toward something greater,
how they always lead somewhere,
even when we cannot see
around the curve.

"Water connects," he'd say.
"It always finds its way to people.
If ever you're lost in the woods,
find water and follow it.
Trust it to lead you home."

I watched him slip
around the bend before me,
carried by the current we both shared.

Now I stood at the curve,
water swirling around my ankles,
unable to see where he had gone—
but knowing the river continued.

Perhaps this rushing silence
was not meant to drown me after all.

Perhaps, like the river,
it was simply carrying us both home—
him beyond the bend I couldn't yet navigate,
me still learning
to trust the flow.

## *The Night of the Waxing Gibbous*

It rained the night you met Him—
not the storming kind,
but the kind where heaven weeps
with reverence.

The air was thick,
not heavy like sorrow,
but dense—
enveloping and close,
like being held too tightly
by time itself.

There were no final words—
only silence,
laced with struggle,
as if breath itself
had become the message.

Throughout the day,
the heavens and I wept together—
tears of sorrow and wonder
braided in aching reverence.

The kind of tears
that rise when love
meets mystery.

Above us,
the waxing gibbous moon stood watch—
not yet full,
but nearly.

A moon in waiting.
A moon that knows something is coming.
It holds light
the way we hold breath—
stretching toward completeness
without rushing it.

And I thought,
how fitting
that on Father's Day,
you went to meet
our Father.

And I believe—
when He gathered you in,
there were tears in His eyes too.

Not of grief,
but of glory.

And maybe, just maybe…
what I saw as drowning—
the breathless letting go,
the silence too vast to name—
was you floating.

Rising.

Teaching me again,
without words,
how to trust the water.

You never lost breath really—
just held it as you went around the bend,
coming up for air beyond the rapids.

And I know, when I finally follow
that same bend in the river,
you'll be waiting—
those sparkly eyes and that mischievous look I know so well—
saying simply:
*"What took you so long?"*

# Acknowledgements

To G. Wray—my covenant love,
my partner in every season—
thank you for being the steady
hand and quiet strength behind
these pages.
You remind me that love, like a
garden, must be tended daily.

To our children and grandchildren —
your lives are the living proof
that love planted well can grow in wonder.
You are each a bloom in the legacy
your grandfather began.

To my siblings,
with whom I share not only
memories, but the soul-soil of childhood—
thank you for the laughter, the ache,
the shared inheritance of love.

To my mother, who left this earth before him,
but not before shaping the soil we
grew in.

To those who have read with me,
wept with me, or walked beside me—
friends, mentors, sacred strangers—
your presence matters more than
you know.

To every reader who meets this story with tenderness—
thank you for walking these paths
with me.

And to the One who sees every seed,
every ache, every unseen blooming—
thank You for the Light that makes
all things grow.

I am so proud of and humbled by
you all.

# About the Author

Gilda Wray is a writer, poet, and
quiet gatherer of stories—
especially the ones that grow in the margins and bloom when
remembered.

She writes to tend the sacred:
presence, memory, and grace.

This book is a tribute and a kept promise—planted long ago in the
garden of her father's love.

It is one of many stories still
growing.

If you've felt something take root
here,
you can find her words in other
quiet places,
or write her directly using the email inside this book.
She'd love to hear what you're
growing, too.